Maison Lesage

Maison Lesage

Haute Couture Embroidery

Patrick Mauriès

Providers of Excellence   *10*

The Birth of Luxury   *14*

A Stroke of Luck   *22*

Handover   *32*

Bias Cut   *36*

Mainteuses and *Lunévilleuses*   *44*

Marie-Louise   *48*

A House is Born   *54*

A Change of Address   *60*

Schiaparelli   *64*

Acrobats and Butterflies   *78*

The Unexpected   *88*

Survival   *94*

Embroidery, Trimmings and Textiles   *100*

François *104*

American Adventures *108*

Return to Paris *114*

Asparagus and Flowers *120*

Old and New Regime *126*

Six Hundred Hours *134*

When Fashion is in Fashion *146*

29 and 92 *154*

A Passage to India *164*

A Long Friendship *172*

Changes *182*

Notes 215   *Picture Credits 216*

Acknowledgments 218   *Index 219*

In the words of Madame Necker, embroidery is to dresses what women are to the art of conversation: 'like the layers of cotton wool we pack into boxes of china, we do not pay much attention to them, but if they were not there everything would fall apart.' It is the ornament that accentuates the line. It adds light and lustre. We might not be consciously aware of it, but like persistence of vision, it leaves an impression on us. And it is meticulously planned, designed and executed.

above A page from Charles-Germain de Saint-Aubin's *L'Art du Brodeur*, 1770

previous pages Michonet, 1868

Since the time of Charles Frederick Worth at the end of the 19th century there have been many big names in the fashion business. But do we know the names of any embroiderers? They are merely the *petites mains*, the artisans without whom the clothes could not be created, but only they know their importance. For a long time they were simply seen as 'providers', playing a subordinate and unobtrusive role. François Lesage ironically turned this around; the title of embroiderer became a mark of respect. In the second half of the 20th century, he became the first to emphasize the role, the name, the 'signature' of the embroiderer. Not to say, however, that some of his predecessors were not keenly aware of the value and creative importance of what is as much an art as a technique. As long ago as 1770, Charles-Germain de Saint-Aubin, the eldest of a family of skilled embroidery artists, published the famous *L'Art du Brodeur*, which formulated, illustrated and codified the various aspects of this age-old craft and raised awareness of its significance, in a similar way to treatises on the art of painting back in the 16th century.

Two hundred years after the publication of Saint-Aubin's treatise, François Lesage's ambition to be not merely an interpreter but a partner of the designers he worked with, his sense of style and the collections of embroidered accessories shown in his own name earned him a place on the Comité Colbert, the body representing the biggest French luxury labels. This was the culmination of a process started by his parents, Albert and Marie-Louise, and continued by his son Jean-François. The story of the Maison Lesage and its many collaborations, from Vionnet to Schiaparelli, from Balenciaga to Saint Laurent, from Christian Lacroix to Chanel, has run parallel to the history of fashion since the early 20th century.

In volume 13 of his *Histoire du Consulat et de l'Empire*, Adolphe Thiers traces the rebirth of luxury in France specifically to the winter of 1802. One of the notable and dramatic effects of the French Revolution and the upheaval it caused was the dissolution of craft guilds. Crafts were no longer passed down from one generation to the next, and skills were lost. According to Henri Baudrillart in his classic work *Histoire du luxe*, Napoleon's desire to revive the pomp of the ruler, the four million spent on his coronation ceremony, the orders for silk from the workshops in Lyon, the silk ordered (for Josephine) from Saint-Quentin, the taste for sumptuous velvets and lamés, and the embroidered robes, benefited from the impetus provided by a ruling regime that virtually made flamboyance its guiding principle.

Baudrillart goes on to say that the three successive exhibitions of products aimed at boosting the economy and production between 1801 and 1806 (after the inaugural exhibition in 1798) had a powerful effect on contemporary society: 'The splendour of gold and silver brocade, satins and velvets, embroidery and braid, trimmings and lace were everywhere.' After a period of upheaval and never-ending destruction, people were longing for peace and the pleasures of luxury.

Various sociological, economic and technological influences contributed to the gradual growth of extravagant expenditure, which, according to Baudrillart, was divided into three periods. In the first wave, between 1815 and 1830, luxury was democratized with the rise of the middle classes and a fall in prices due to early forms of mechanical reproduction (mahogany veneer, papier-mâché). The second period, from 1830 to 1848, was notable for its spirit of romantic imagination but it was also a time of bourgeois eclecticism, imitating styles from antiquity to the Middle Ages, then from the 17th century to the 18th-century pompadour. According to Baudrillart, it was 'a sort of juxtaposition of all periods, bearing no relation to the needs of our era'. The third period, from 1848 to 1872, was a time of steady expansion, with material prosperity, the rapid acquisition of wealth, and money being lavished on pleasure. It culminated in the extraordinary opulence of the Second Empire, which spread through all sectors of society. In the words of Baudrillart, citing Balzac, Chateaubriand, Dumas and Lamartine: 'I would venture to say that at no time in history has the idea of luxury been so prominent in the works and lives of famous writers.'

New demand called for special suppliers and special craftsmen. The Baccarat glassworks reinvented itself in 1816 and the most famous French luxury brands began to appear: Christofle in

opposite Michonet, 1884

previous pages Michonet, 1921

1830, Hermès in 1837, Vuitton in 1854. These laid the foundations for what was to become the latest and perhaps longest-lasting expression of extravagant excess: Haute Couture, with the opening of Charles Frederick Worth's salon in 1858. Jacques Doucet took over the family business at 21 rue de la Paix in 1875, Redfern was established in Paris in 1881, Paquin at 3 rue de la Paix ten years later and Callot Soeurs at 24 rue Taitbout in 1895. A new sector opened up and became permanent, part of the very definition of Parisian luxury.

Worth might be seen as the instigator of the butterfly effect that eventually led to the Maison Lesage. The first of the great couturiers was less a master of line – he did not try to redraw it but merely accentuated it, dividing the body into two halves around a cinched-in waist – than a virtuoso of opulence, of rich materials and textures. It was a perfect reflection of the spirit of the age, the 19th-century taste mentioned by Walter Benjamin, characterized by layering and combining, a proliferation of trimmings, insets, overlays, quilting, cut-out and openwork effects. A whole vocabulary for furnishings and clothes emerged, with passementerie as the common feature. This trend was also mentioned by Baudrillart, who curiously ascribed moral connotations to it ('in the group of threads and fabrics, so many ornaments, trimmings, embroidery, buttons, fringes, novelties, which I am not disparaging, but their excess does not help to encourage economy by the poor or virtuous behaviour by the rich'). Day and evening gowns were weighed down with chenille, tassels, frogging, silk trimmings, velvet panels, jet bugles, glass beads, decorative flowers, plus of course the traditional lace and embroidery. As Palmer White writes in his book on Lesage: 'Under Worth's impetus, embroidery evolved so actively that forty embroidery houses mushroomed almost overnight.'

Among those workshops, the atelier of a young embroiderer, Albert Michonet, was noted for its high standards, supplying not only Worth but most of the major fashion houses with what was by then known as couture up until the 1920s. This was when, as we shall see, the butterfly Lesage emerged from the Michonet chrysalis.

opposite   Michonet, late 19th century

overleaf   Michonet, 1904

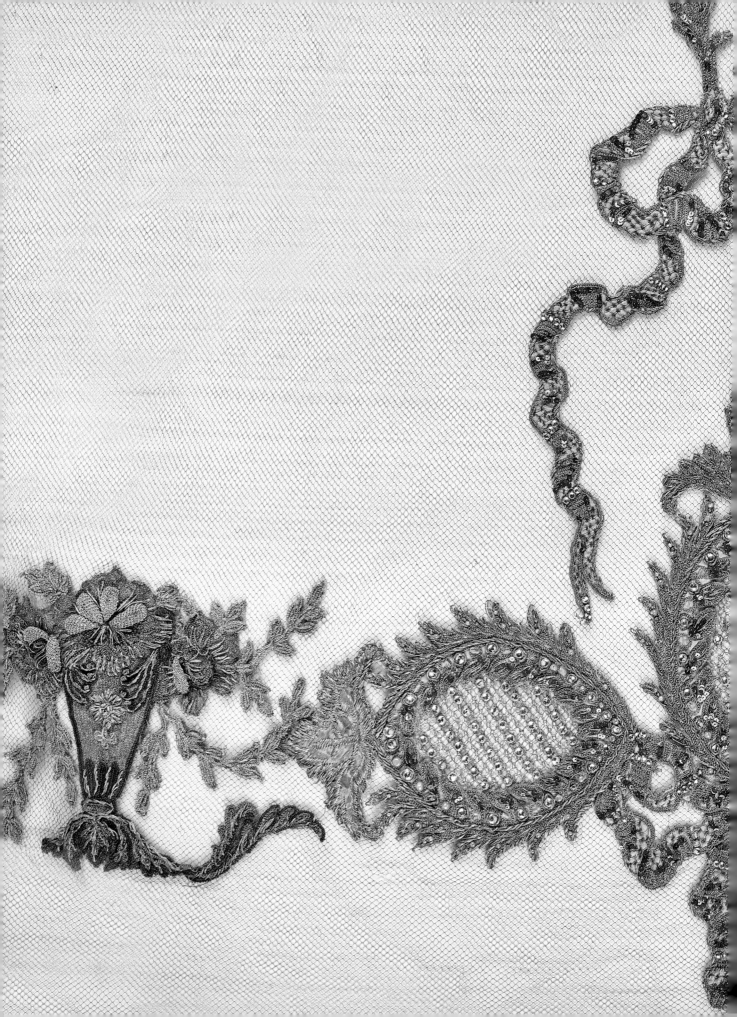

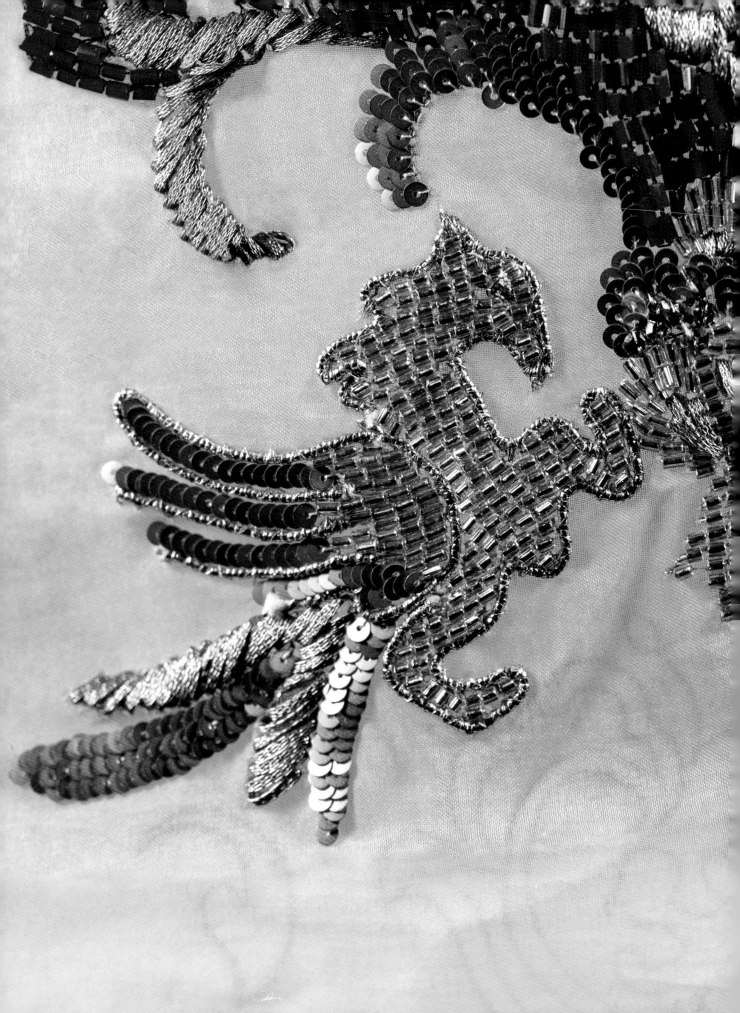

Originally from Normandy, the Lesage family settled in Lorraine after the Revolution. Driven from their land by the German annexation of 1871, François's grandparents Adèle and Gustave Lesage fled to Paris. They lived on rue Fontaine near the Place Pigalle, in a working-class district that was being rapidly modernized (the introduction of town gas at that time dramatically altered the area, along with the building of new streets). A quiet and reserved man, an archivist at the publishing house Hachette, Gustave had a passion for drawing and every Sunday he would go to the gardens at Saint-Cloud to sketch from nature. That was something he had in common with his son Albert. Adèle appears to have been content in her traditional role as a housewife.

above   Albert Lesage, Chicago, 1920

previous pages   Michonet, 1921

Albert Lesage was born in 1888. He was a good student, finishing school and showing an aptitude for languages. At the age of twenty-two, after three years of military service, he had to find a job. He was taken on by a foreign trade agency, brokers who passed on, negotiated and executed purchase and sale orders on behalf of third parties, often abroad. The agency worked particularly for large American stores and dress houses, which at the time did not send buyers to the biannual Paris fashion shows but relied on these agents to deal with suppliers and couture firms for them. This was Albert Lesage's introduction to the world he was to work in for the rest of his life.

This smooth career path was brought to an abrupt halt four years later by the outbreak of the First World War. Early in the war Albert was wounded in the German attack on the Meuse. He was taken prisoner and sent to the Merseburg camp, in the south of Saxony-Anhalt, spending more than four years there as one of 10,000 French prisoners. He left a wealth of pictorial evidence of those long years in captivity, in the form of drawings, watercolours and caricatures providing a detailed record of his daily life, as well as countless variations on an imaginary female figure, a combination of an ideal woman and a fashion model.

On returning to France at the beginning of 1919, Albert went back to his former job but he now found it restrictive. As luck would have it, however, a family friend, Simone Bouvet de Lozier, who had made a name as a designer on Fifth Avenue, used Albert's firm as her agents. Impressed by the young man's drawings and seeing that he was dissatisfied in his current job, she decided to help him by showing his sketches to the director of Marshall Field and Company, a Chicago department store that was another of the agency's clients. A few weeks later, Albert was offered a job as a manager and designer in the women's department of the store.

Barely six months after his return to France, Albert sailed to America at the age of thirty-one, opening a new chapter in his life. According to Palmer White (who probably learned this from François Lesage), Albert had another stroke of luck on the voyage, which only came to light in the course of a conversation fifteen years later. An aristocratic couple, Count William Wendt de Kerlor and his young wife from a good Roman family, were travelling on the upper decks of Albert's ship. She was captivated by what was described as the magnetic gaze of her exotic companion. Years later, having reverted to her maiden name, she was to play a key role in the history of fashion and in the life of Albert Lesage.

This stay in the United States had a profound effect on the ideas and approaches of the two future collaborators. They found an economy, a dynamic and a fashion distribution system that were completely different from what they were used to, and they went on to exploit their new experiences successfully. Albert had to satisfy the requirements of both middle-class clients in Chicago and society women with 'new money', mostly from trade and industry. The compromise was only partly successful. An original is always better than a copy, no matter how good. 'By the time Albert was thirty-four', says Palmer White, 'he had perfected his English, learned a great deal about business organization and its methods as the Americans practised them, and saved a tidy sum of dollars. He felt that life, love and happiness should be pursued elsewhere.'

opposite and pages 28–31 Michonet, late 19th century

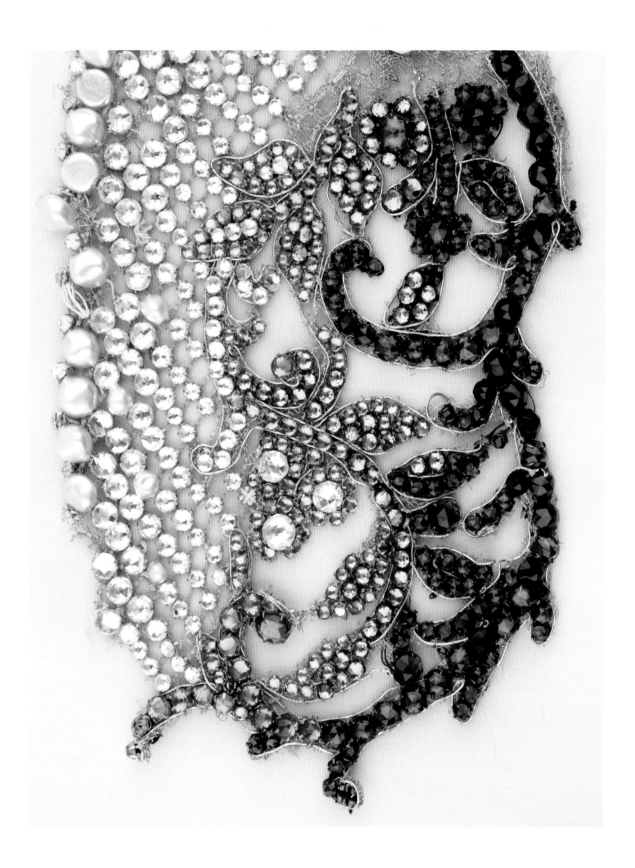

The Paris that Albert returned to in 1922 had changed dramatically. Paris fashion had established a reputation and American clients were starting to travel or send their buyers to see the collections at first hand. They would then buy prototypes through agencies, a system that has continued to this day.

At the same time, the intellectual and artistic scene was going through a turbulent period. The controversial Dada movement began in 1916, the ballet *Parade* caused a scandal the following year, the orientalism of the Ballets Russes in its early days gave way to avant-garde provocation, André Breton published his *Surrealist Manifesto* in 1924 and a year later the Exhibition of Decorative Arts in Paris became the catalyst for a new sensibility in the field of applied arts. The fifteen-year period before the Second World War was a time of extraordinary creativity, marked by a series of artistic movements and counter-movements, and those trends, which were more than just theoretical, would have a direct effect on Albert Lesage's career.

In that changing society, Worth's star faded and he was supplanted by Poiret, before Poiret too gave way to the modern understatement of Chanel and Patou. The line was streamlined, fabrics became more fluid, decoration was redesigned. According to Palmer White, of the dozens of embroidery ateliers of the Belle Époque period, only twenty-two survived, including the firm of Albert Michonet, which was able to adapt and meet the requirements of the new fashion houses and so continued to flourish. As the sole head of his firm, now getting on in years, Michonet was keen to retire but at the same time reluctant to see the results of so much work and creativity disappear. Methodically he compiled an archive of swatches and designs that was capital in itself, and the firm was financially and commercially sound. His clients included Paquin, Doucet and Redfern, as well as members of the aristocracy and royal families. His highly accomplished motifs could be used for both passementerie and theatrical costumes.

Albert Lesage had savings from his time in the United States and, realizing the situation, he arranged a meeting with Michonet, whose atelier was then on rue Feydeau behind the Bibliothèque Nationale. They came to a provisional agreement in the autumn of 1922. They would start their collaboration with a six-month trial period before entering into a real partnership, then the firm would be sold within eighteen months. Given the economic climate, which was to have disastrous long-term consequences, this was a shrewd move by Albert. The speculation against the franc starting in early 1924, which led to the emergence of the Coalition of the Left in May, increased the value of his dollar assets by nearly 300 per cent by the time the sale was decided. Furthermore, the trial period proved successful. But one of the unforeseen consequences of the deal was to play an even more decisive part in the advent of the Maison Lesage. A distant descendant of the Spencer family, which made the news in a different way later in the century, and one of the greatest couturiers in the history of fashion were the unwitting participants.

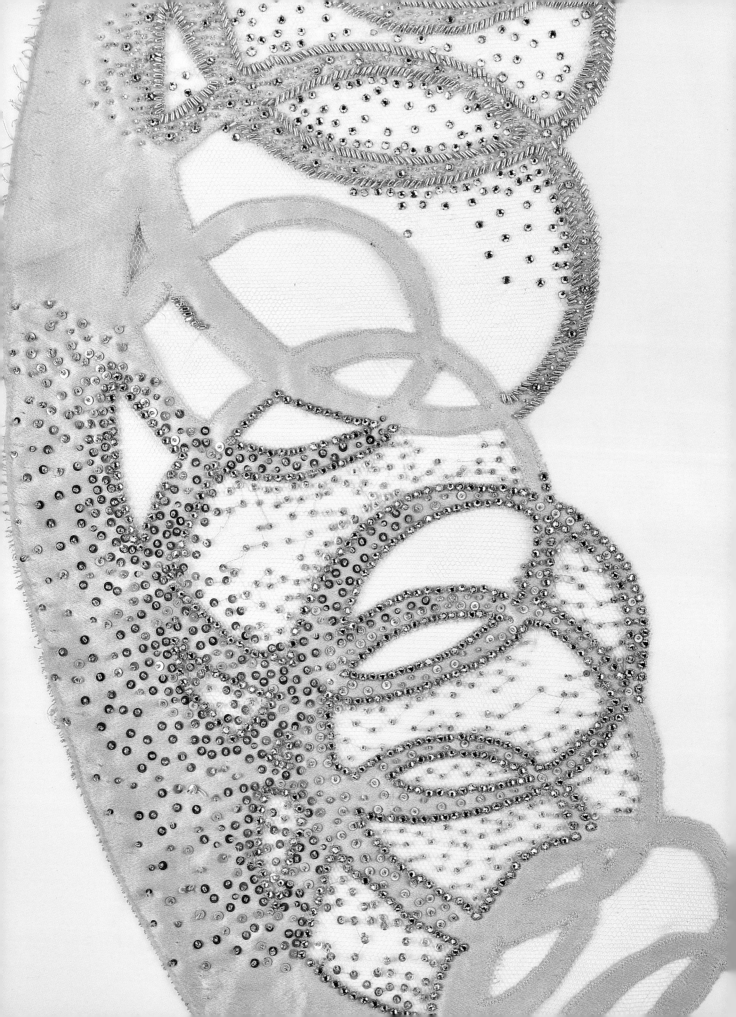

Like Cristóbal Balenciaga and Azzedine Alaïa in later years, Madeleine Vionnet was one of the rare figures in the history of fashion who knew how to cut, stitch and assemble a garment. Born in the Loiret in 1876, she followed her family to Aubervilliers in the suburbs of Paris. She started her apprenticeship in a modest dressmaking workshop at the age of thirteen. Once she had learned the basics, she joined the couturier Vincent on rue de la Paix in Paris in 1890. Unusually independent for the time, she travelled to England when she was not yet eighteen and led a hand-to-mouth existence before finding a job with a dressmaker in London's Dover Street, Kate Reily. There she trained in the strict cutting techniques of the English tailors. On returning to Paris in 1900, she was employed as head seamstress by Callot Soeurs, one of the leading fashion houses, where she 'worked particularly with Madame Gerber,' writes Palmer White, 'the eldest of the three sisters, a great perfectionist.'

above Madeleine Vionnet, 1930

previous pages Vionnet, 1938

Five years later, she received an offer from another leading couturier, Jacques Doucet, on the recommendation of one of his former designers, Paul Poiret. Poiret had originally been offered the job but was not interested at the time. Impressed by Vionnet's fashion sense and knowledge, Doucet soon allowed her more scope and she immediately started working on her recurring themes: fluidity and draped fabrics (later copied by Madame Grès), freeing the body from constraints. It was a complete departure from what was still the current fashion, allowing her to challenge Poiret's claim that it was he who had abolished the corset.

Her creations were so well-received that she was able to set up on her own and open her first shop at 222 rue de Rivoli in 1912. It was immediately successful. The outbreak of war two years later forced her to close, but she reopened at the end of the war with the support of a wealthy financier. She never stopped working, and in 1926 she perfected the process that was emblematic of her style: soft light fabrics, cut on the bias to emphasize their sculptural nature.

That innovation also made her a pioneer in another way. Her creations were so often borrowed, copied and adapted that she found herself at the centre of a famous copyright case, which she won. She restricted production of her designs and even released certificates of authenticity, marked with her fingerprint. Designing nearly 600 creations a year, Vionnet, according to Palmer White, constantly 'sought to perfect the flowing lines, balance and aerial appearance that were magical in her hands. To enhance the purity of the flow, she inclined towards soft fabrics, principally chiffon and crêpe de Chine. She favoured monochrome – off-white, ivory, cream, beige, pale green – and used few strong colours save the "Vionnet red", a sun-drenched terracotta, deep green and, of course, black. She would not permit a dart to be seen ... a woman slipped her head through the top of a Vionnet gown and it dropped softly about her, occasionally fastened by hooks or pop-fasteners, never by a zip.'

overleaf, left   Vionnet, Little Horses dress, 1921
overleaf, right   Vionnet, 1937
page 42   Vionnet, bias-cut evening gown, 1935
page 43   Vionnet, 1925

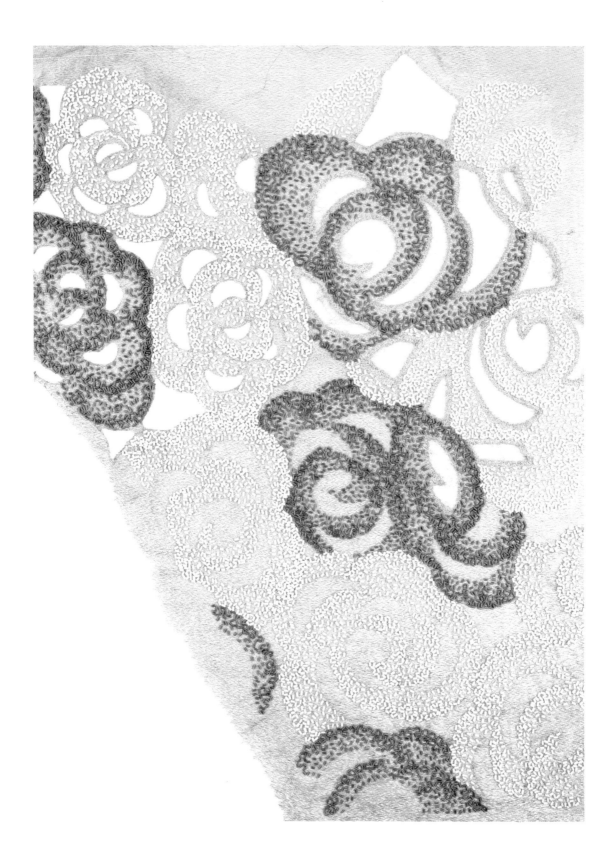

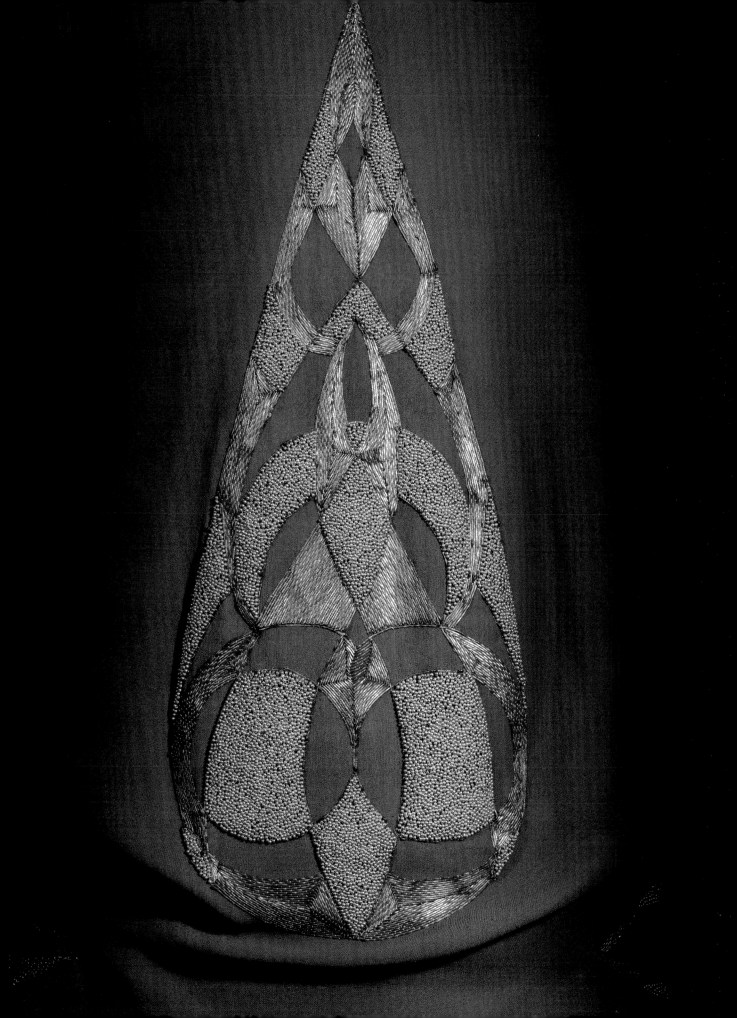

Garlands, bouquets or chains of roses winding around the body as a counterpoint to the simplicity of the line were another recurring motif in Vionnet's creations. Bias-cut in shaded silk muslin, braided with silk embroidery, these delicate fabric flowers were just one of the challenges facing Michonet in meeting Madeleine Vionnet's expectations. He was the embroiderer she used to design and make trimmings and adornments suited to her favourite fabrics. The style had completely changed; now it was essential for the fluid bias-cut chiffon and crêpe not to be weighed down with heavy materials like beads, fringing and jet. And design, colours and textures had to be altered, brought into line with the spirit of modernity whose leading designers Vionnet admired and collected, from Jean Dunand (she adapted his colours) to Pierre Chareau and Jean-Michel Frank.

above left   Pouncing materials
above right   Lunéville beading

previous pages   Embroidery sample

This had a direct effect on working methods and incidentally leads on to an important and little-known aspect of the embroiderer's art. Needle in hand, threading beads, sequins and rhinestones before stitching them onto the fabric, embroiderers traditionally used to sew on their ornaments, whether precious stones, fake gems or plastic strips, one after another in a long and painstaking process. These needle embroiderers were known in the trade as *mainteuses*.

But in the first half of the 19th century, workers in Lunéville invented a new system that saved on work, time and costs, using a small hook as well as a needle. The technique became known as Lunéville or tambour beading. First, the beads or sequins are loaded onto a thread. Working from the 'wrong' side of the fabric, which is stretched across a frame, the embroiderer uses the needle to position the threaded beads on the right side and then attaches them to the reverse side, using the hook. This was much quicker than the method used by the *mainteuses* and at first they were strongly opposed to it. In particular, it allowed very delicate materials such as sequins, bugles and other tiny beads to be attached very precisely. The fashion for beaded flapper dresses in the 1920s and the need to meet the growing demand encouraged the initial boom in Lunéville embroidery. It offered Albert Lesage a method that was perfectly suited to the requirements of Madeleine Vionnet's style. Subtle patterns could be created on the flowing and delicate fabrics – chiffon, crêpe and silk gauze – that she favoured. It also allowed Albert to demonstrate his creativity and introduce countless innovations. But he could not have done it without the help of another key figure in the history of the firm, whom Madeleine Vionnet happened to bring to the Michonet atelier one day while Albert was there.

Perhaps only the expert ear of a genealogist would recognize the connection between the name Despense and the English name Spencer. A married couple from the eminent Spencer family arrived in France in the retinue of Mary, Queen of Scots in 1558 and changed their name to Despense, which they thought sounded much better to the French ear. Ennobled by Mary and rewarded with the estate of Railly in Burgundy, these Spencers reinvented themselves as Comte and Comtesse de Despense-Railly.

Three centuries later, Berthe de Despense-Railly, whose fortunes had faded, fell in love with her cousin Paul Favot from Chevannes and, after marrying her suitor, left the modest family manor house to live in Auteuil, where she took charge of the household and, in particular, home dressmaking. In 1895 she had a daughter, who inherited her mother's skills and artistic sense.

above   Marie-Louise Lesage, 1922

previous pages   Michonet, early 20th century
overleaf   Vionnet, 1930

After a sound education, Marie-Louise quickly developed a sense of form and colour, and a talent for drawing. After finishing secondary school, she passed the entrance exam for the École Nationale des Arts Décoratifs. Her four years there before she graduated coincided with the First World War, her father's mobilization and some financial difficulties. To support the family, she had to help her mother with her dressmaking and she learned how to cut, fit and finish a garment.

At the end of the war, after finishing her studies, Marie-Louise had to decide what to do and chose fashion. After hesitating between the two most prestigious names, Paul Poiret and Madeleine Vionnet, she went to the latter's atelier at 222 rue de Rivoli and was employed on the spot. To distinguish herself from the many people with similar names in the atelier, she decided to use a resonant and clear syllable – 'Yo' – as a nickname, which stayed with her for the rest of her life. Her job was to collect documents and sources of inspiration for the designer, and she also helped to develop the designs. Palmer White writes: 'Like Poiret before her and Alix (later Grès) afterwards, [Vionnet] draped fabrics on a miniature wooden dummy, and on a customer once an order had been received. Upon conceiving a gown, she asked Marie-Louise to sketch on cotton canvas the place that an embroidery was to occupy.'

While today's designers tell the embroiderer the motif or theme they want or, alternatively, base their designs on swatches provided by the embroiderer, at Vionnet the embroidery had to be planned, designed and applied to the garment at the atelier. It was up to Marie-Louise in particular to make sure that Michonet reproduced the patterns correctly, that the tones and colours were true to the design. So she often had to go to rue Feydeau to check the work of the embroiderers, and it was during one such visit that Albert Michonet introduced her to the young man with whom he had just signed a partnership agreement, who would later take over the firm. Palmer White records that it was love at first sight, and they were married a few months later with the support of Simone Bouvet de Lozier, who had encouraged Albert to go to the United States. She travelled from New York for the occasion.

VIONNET OCT. 1930
4233

There was no question of Marie-Louise giving up work. She was still deeply independent and left Madeleine Vionnet, who was at the peak of her profession and had around 1,200 employees, only to follow her husband to Michonet and focus on her connection with the person who had been the first to place trust in her. Apart from their personal relationship, Marie-Louise and Albert Lesage seemed to complement each other naturally. He was a designer with an entrepreneurial spirit and American experience; she had a feel for colour, an artistic background and imagination. Marie-Louise also had the advantage of already being familiar with embroidery techniques and the working methods of the atelier on

top left François Lesage with his older brother Jean-Louis and twin sister Christiane
top right Elisabeth, Countess Greffulhe, in a Worth gown, *c.* 1900
above Lesage family

previous pages Worth, 1944

rue Feydeau. In the interim eighteen months provided for in the transfer agreement, Albert and Marie-Louise had ample time to explore the firm's impressive archive, its collections of swatches and designs dating back more than fifty years, and to share Albert Michonet's exceptional experience.

At the same time, they needed to follow the spirit of the age and take account of the changing tastes of which Vionnet's fashions were just one symptom. As mentioned, Lesage's acquisition of Michonet benefited from the economic situation in 1924 and it took place just one year before the real revolution, Paris's 1925 Exhibition of Decorative Arts, which saw the crystallization of a genuinely new style, Art Deco. Vionnet shared the decorative repertoire of the artists and creators whose works she collected, with a preference for flat surfaces, simple, geometric, abstract, organic forms, often with broken lines.

We have seen how Vionnet's cutting methods and the fabrics she favoured had a direct effect on the design, elements and even the texture of the embroidery. Albert and Marie-Louise had to innovate immediately to respond to this new style. They improved the vermicelli technique in which a sinuous network of tiny beads was sewn using the Lunéville method into an increasingly dense pattern, which called for exceptional skill on the part of the embroiderer. They used irregular glass beads, tube seeds, plant fibres steamed and covered with beads. To make the embroidery as delicate as possible, they also invented a shading technique in which the embroidered pattern was plunged inch by inch into a bath of increasingly strong dye, then put back on the dress, creating an ombré effect. This became one of the firm's specialities. Taking the perfectionism even further, as Palmer White writes, Albert 'went so far as to use a logarithm table to calculate the design of a length of embroidery in relation to the fall of a gown', but he also knew how to turn accidents and unforeseen circumstances to his advantage. One day, a box of sequins was accidentally dropped onto one of the atelier's coal-fired stoves, causing the sequins to puff up like popcorn. Lesage liked the effect and went on to use these 'soufflé' beads in embroidery designs for Madeleine Vionnet and Elsa Schiaparelli.

For more than fifteen years Lesage worked with Madeleine Vionnet in her unstoppable rise, as she established a business on Fifth Avenue, opened a salon in Biarritz and set up a training institute; at its peak in the 1930s, the fashion house occupied a five-storey building on avenue Montaigne with twenty-one workshops as well as doctor's and dentist's surgeries, another sign of Vionnet's concern for the welfare of her staff. Lesage created over 1,500 designs for the couturière, until the day in August 1939 when, well aware of the looming catastrophe, she showed her last collection. She would live for another thirty-five years, leading a very quiet life but ensuring her place in the history of fashion, particularly by means of a large legacy to the Musée des Arts Décoratifs. The sheer scale of her collaboration with Lesage was enough to leave an indelible mark on the history of the firm, only equalled a little later by the work with another designer with a much less restrained style.

Vionnet, evening gown, 1929

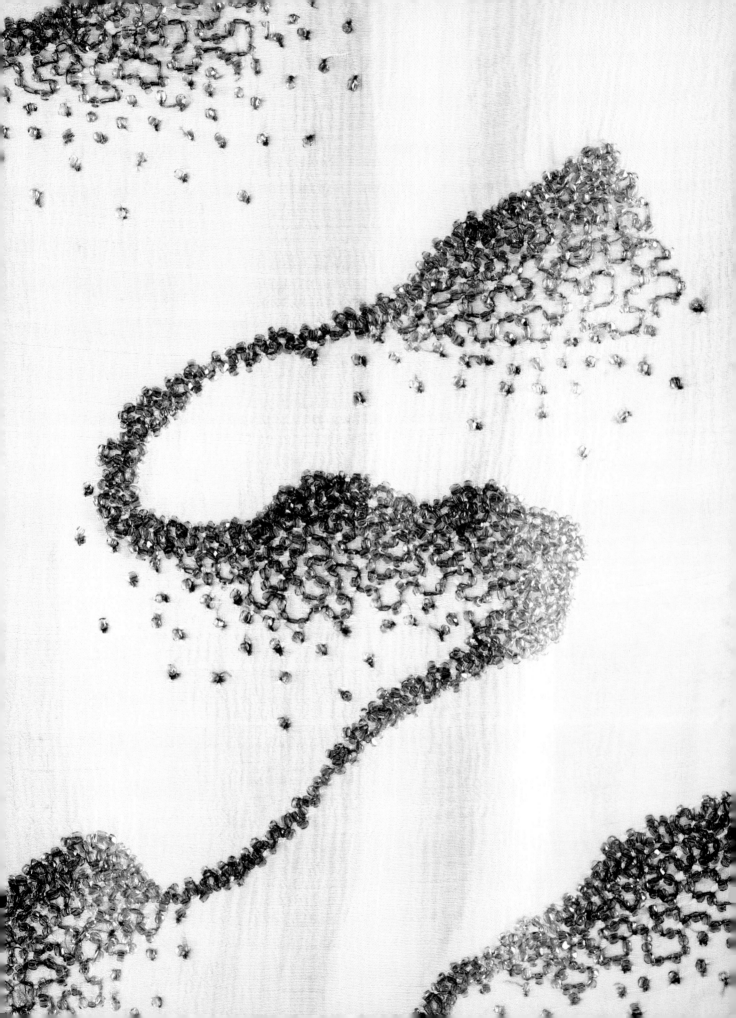

François Lesage was born on 31 March 1929, a few hours before his twin sister Christiane. They remained close in spite of their very different lives. Their elder brother Jean-Louis, born five years earlier, was already the great hope of the family despite his poor health. The Lesages had just gone through a period of prosperity and had moved to an old house in Chaville, which would remain the family's gathering place for several generations.

As agreed, Albert Lesage et Cie had taken over Michonet in 1924 and the future seemed bright. Until the day in October 1929, just a few months after the birth of the twins, when the New York stock exchange collapsed, the first stage in a chain reaction that would shatter the world economy. The fashion industry lost its American clients overnight. The major fashion houses saw their turnover drastically reduced. Their suppliers – shoemakers, dressmakers, suppliers of feather and leather work, furriers – were the first to suffer the effects of the crisis, and embroiderers were not immune (6,000 were laid off in Lunéville alone).

Demonstrating one of the traits that would be passed on to the firm, his inventiveness, flexibility and quick responses, Albert Lesage looked for new opportunities. He moved away from conventional dress codes, for instance using a simpler form of embroidery on clothes of a kind that were not yet known as sportswear. He also made an inconclusive attempt to move into fabric prints, which were then very fashionable, but he was less successful in this than the silk makers of the time, Bianchini in particular. Another initiative, which was slightly more profitable, was to use the embroidery and passementerie resources to develop a line of accessories, belts, bags and costume jewelry, which added a decorative touch to the line of a garment. This natural extension of the Maison's work would be taken up again by François half a century later, this time with great success.

Albert had to cut back his team and be pragmatic in his approach: 'Now to maintain even a skeleton staff of embroideresses,' Palmer White writes, 'extreme measures had to be taken. The bookkeeper swept the floors and dusted, Marie-Louise handled the correspondence, Albert himself ran the errands. In 1929 there had been twenty embroidery houses, now only ten remained. Increasingly anxious, Albert came to fear that soon there would only be nine.' (It was the same situation that his son François faced in the early 1980s, with the advent of luxury Prêt-à-Porter. The dominant aesthetic shunned adornment and there was little call for embroidery. That was another critical time for the Maison, as we shall see.)

But even in hard times, fortune seemed to smile on Albert. Just as circumstances and the devaluation of the franc had worked in his favour at the time of the Michonet acquisition, when he was forced to leave rue Feydeau in 1931 as a result of a property deal, he managed to turn the situation to his advantage. Exploiting the impatience of the developers, he raised the bidding, and that enabled him to move his now smaller team to 13 rue de la Grange-Batelière, where some of the firm's work is still done today. But it was above all the unexpected telephone call in 1934 from a true *deus ex machina*, the former Comtesse Wendt de Kerlor, that helped him out of the situation.

opposite and previous pages   Vionnet, 1938

Since she and Albert had crossed the Atlantic on the same ship in 1919, Elsa Wendt de Kerlor had lost her title and her illusions about her husband (his aristocratic background was somewhat suspect; in fact, he had simply joined together the surnames of his parents). Initially they had shared an interest in the occult, magic and other theosophical ideas, and she was so fascinated by him that she had even become his hypnotic subject. But she had eventually tired of the unstable relationship, the constant moves, the visits by bailiffs and the precarious lifestyle. After the premature death of an up-and-coming opera singer with whom she had had a brief

above Elsie de Wolfe, Lady Mendl, wearing the Apollo of Versailles cape
from Schiaparelli's Astrology collection. Photograph by Cecil Beaton, late 1930s

opposite Schiaparelli, Apollo of Versailles cape, Astrology collection, 1938
previous pages Schiaparelli, Circus collection, 1938

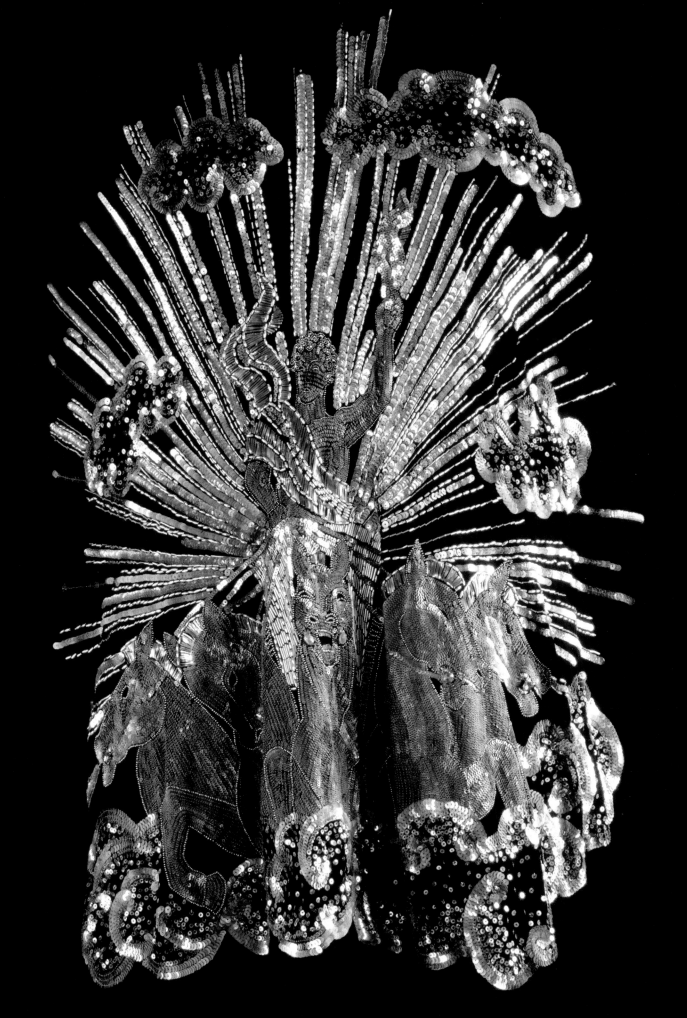

Elsa Schiaparelli by Christian Bérard, given to François Lesage
by Schiaparelli before he left for the United States, 1946

romance, Madame de Kerlor decided to revert to her maiden name, Schiaparelli, and return to Europe with her daughter, nicknamed Gogo, the only positive outcome of her marriage.

She returned to Paris in 1922. In the company of Gabrielle Buffet-Picabia, a female friend who was also separated, she was immediately plunged into literary and artistic society, meeting all the right people, from Tzara to Duchamp to Cocteau, and being seen in all the right places. When Paul Poiret saw her at his private theatre and noticed how stylishly she dressed, he gave her some of his creations to wear free of charge. According to her biographer Meryle Secrest, she was complimented by the great couturier on an evening outfit that had been more or less improvised for her friend Gabrielle, and was suddenly launched, without even realizing it, into the world that would become hers for over thirty years.

Her first creation was a sweater with three-quarter sleeves and a trompe-l'œil bow, shaped in a way that would ensure a good fit. It stood out from those of her competitors because of its texture and the use of a motif on a garment that had previously been seen as purely functional. Meryle Secrest writes that it was 'a way of dressing that bridged the gulf between the casual and the dressy'. It was an instant success, hailed in the December 1927 issue of *Vogue* as 'an artistic masterpiece and a triumph of colour blending'. This creation nearly a century ago foreshadowed the work of many present-day designers and was the first in a series of innovations. The seamless dresses, one-piece bathing costumes and 'mad cap' (a little two-pointed hat) were a commercial success, making money for their creator and enabling her to set up her own fashion house with the support of Charles Kahn of Galeries Lafayette in December 1927.

This first sweater designed by Schiaparelli incorporated most of the features of her later designs. She designed for a fairly slim female form, unconstrained, with fluid lines. The way we define the look of a 'modern' woman today was established as early as 1932, strongly influenced by Chanel and Patou.

Schiaparelli blurred the boundaries between day and evening wear. The clothes were designed to be easy to wear and allow freedom of movement; for instance, she opened up a straight skirt with two large fan-shaped slits. She was not an expert cutter like Vionnet and she did not aim to revolutionize the structure of the garment. Her work was more in the nature of a chance encounter, an effect, a wink, a hint of seduction. It was a style that you might expect from this upper-class Roman, tending towards the baroque. It was certainly consistent with her artistic friendships (and collaborations) with Salvador Dalí and Jean Cocteau, Christian Bérard and Marcel Vertès, Léonor Fini and Francis Picabia.

Paradoxically, at a time when many fashion houses were closing and the crisis was starting, Schiaparelli's firm was still an enormous success. She had extended her empire from New York to London and Paris. At the beginning of 1935 she was able to leave the premises at 4 rue de la Paix, which she had occupied since 1927, and move to a 98-room private house in Place Vendôme that would remain her historic headquarters.

opposite   Schiaparelli, Astrology collection, 1938

overleaf, left   Schiaparelli, 'Cocteau' evening coat, based on a design by Jean Cocteau, 1937
overleaf, right   Illustration of the 'Cocteau' evening coat by Cecil Beaton for *Vogue*, 1937
page 74   Design by Jean Cocteau for a Schiaparelli evening jacket, 1937
page 75   Schiaparelli, 'Cocteau' evening jacket, 1937
page 76   Schiaparelli, evening blouse, Astrology collection, 1938
page 77   Schiaparelli, Pagan collection, 1938

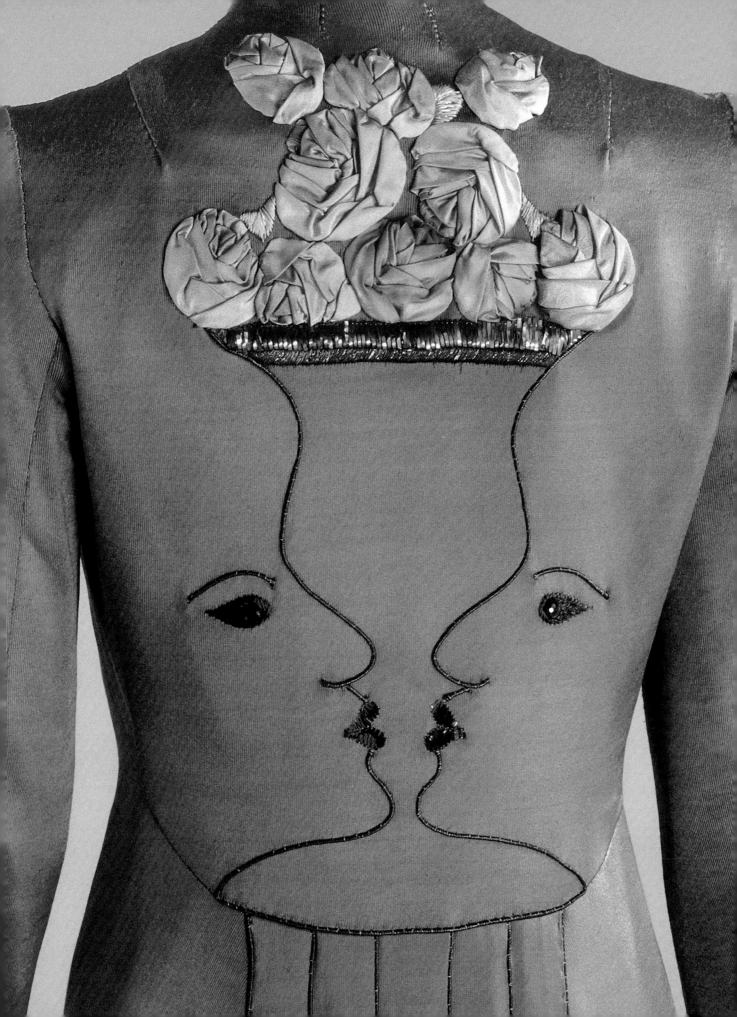

Robe de Schiaparelli - 1937.

orné par Jean Cocteau.

Schiaparelli

A gray linen dress embroidered
with Cocteau's design—hair golden,
lips pink, eyes peacock blue,
and a blue Cellophane hand-
kerchief. Hattie Carnegie.

Chanel

White marocain twinkling with
black paillettes, a black ribbon
belt and a mad coiffure con-
cocted of ribbon, feathers and
a pailletted veil. Salon de
Couture, Bonwit Teller.

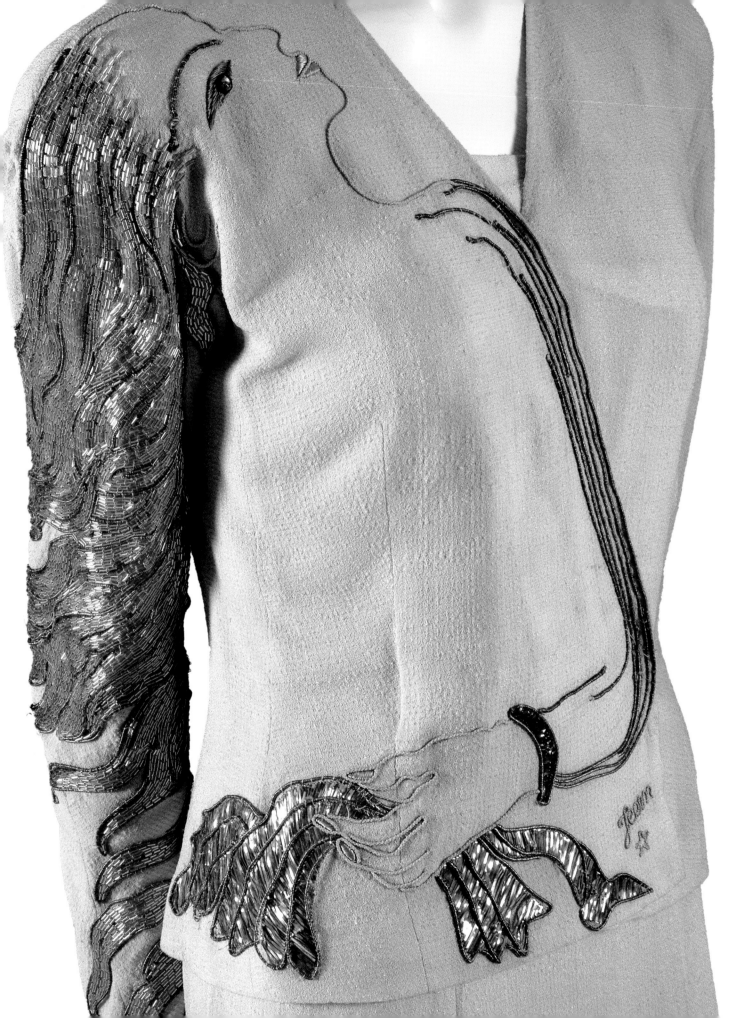

When Schiaparelli approached Lesage in 1934, it was of course with the aim of extending her decorative repertoire, which was then restricted to a small amount of braids and trimmings, and adding something to her designs that would make them stand out. But she also wanted to give some discreet help to the atelier, which she knew was in difficulties owing to her membership of the trade association, the Chambre Syndicale de la Haute Couture. As a trial run, she ordered a series of embroidered belts from Albert and Marie-Louise, incorporating magnificent gold thread passementerie, set with large cabochons of coral and turquoise. These were followed by a collection of necklaces, yokes and collars, which led to more garments – suits, dresses, coats, boleros and fantastical capes. Lesage's relationship with the couturière became closer and closer, only ending when Schiaparelli closed down twenty years later.

The Lesages had an inventive and experimental approach that enabled them to adapt to the baroque, vibrant, playful and individual style of the Italian couturière, just as they had to the understated and subtle creations of Madeleine Vionnet at the other extreme. 'Albert introduced materials into his embroidery', Palmer White says, 'that were equally imaginative: Murano-blown glass for little flowers; imitations of hard minerals – lapis lazuli, jade, turquoise matrix with a little black filament; glass stones and beach pebbles, cabochons and so on. He crushed gelatine beads to lend them the appearance of hammered coins and combined chenille with of all things grand, mink. At Schiaparelli's behest, Albert brought back into fashion bullion (*cannetille*), a spiral-twisted metal thread, and then employed metal to reflect its new uses as demonstrated by the Arts Déco exhibition that had wrought such an impact on her and led to her introducing into fashion many of the new substances of the modern industrial world – plastics, latex, cellophane, rayon crêpe, tulle and knits.'

In contrast to the fluid, finely grained embroidery favoured by Vionnet, Schiaparelli emphasized the three-dimensional, tactile nature of the decoration. Fabrics were given a sense of relief: instead of discreet vermicelli applied using the Lunéville technique, she used 'thistle' and 'hedgehog' textures that took their inspiration from ecclesiastical and military garments, made by hand with traditional padded and quilted techniques: twisted gold braid, smooth gold thread, hammered or embossed, reflecting the light, set with mirror fragments and semi-precious stones.

Until the outbreak of war, this complete rapport between designer and embroiderer resulted in a series of memorable collections that would grant Schiaparelli a permanent place in the history of fashion. After the relative success of the Eskimo collection in October 1935 and the Parachute collection in February 1936, the Music collection set the tone a year later: jewelry, belts and necklaces in the shape of drums, mandolins and bagpipes were coupled with long silk crêpe dresses embroidered with songbirds and musical notes rendered in ribbons and beads. These were followed by the four 1938 collections, which were unanimously considered to be Schiaparelli's and also Albert Lesage's best-ever creations.

opposite Schiaparelli, Pagan collection, 1938

previous pages Schiaparelli, 1939
overleaf, left Schiaparelli, Phoebus cape, 1938–1939
overleaf, right Schiaparelli's Phoebus cape, illustrated by Christian Bérard for *Vogue*, 1938

The Circus collection shown in February 1938 was an extraordinary spectacle. Tightrope walkers and acrobats mingled with the graceful parade of mannequins. Bérard left a superb record of the occasion in his illustrations for *Vogue*, not surprisingly because it was also one of his favourite subjects and he may well have been actively involved in the designer's choice and execution of the theme. The collection was Schiaparelli's take on a theme that Picasso had explored early in the century, presenting a dazzling series of variations on traditional circus costumes. Shocking pink clowns' hats, ringmasters' sequinned jackets, riders' top hats and brilliantly coloured satin boleros were paired with a profusion of embroidery in the same style: acrobats, trapeze artists, performing horses, elephant roundabouts, and so on. Even the buttons and jewelry (designed by Jean Schlumberger) took the shapes of clown faces, barley sugar, liquorice, candy floss or dancing horses. Schiaparelli embraced a subject that would remain a constant in her creations, even in the advertisements for her perfumes illustrated by Bérard and, most famously, Vertès.

The Pagan collection in April 1938 explored the plant motifs for which Schiaparelli and her poet friend Lise Deharme shared a great liking. The theme was a mythical forest peopled with elves and classical gods: 'Wood nymphs wore jackets buttoned with owls, stag's heads, nuts, brightly feathered birds and insects. Belts of supple foliage encircled their waists, bright twigs entwined their bosoms as embroidery, wound about their arms forming multiple bracelets, and nestled in their hair as clips, while ferns adorned their lapels.' To add depth and brilliance to the arabesques of foliage twining around the bodies and the embroidered flowers, Albert combined matt metallic thread with lamé openwork and sequins.

Three months later, the Astrology collection continued to build on Schiaparelli's interest in esotericism, the occult and astrology, using every facet of celestial mythology and the elemental forces. The moon, the sun, the stars and the planets have always been an inexhaustible source of ornamental motifs, but in this collection they gave the designer and the embroiderer an opportunity to create something mythical. Particularly notable were the sequinned sun radiating across a shocking pink woollen cape and a burst of gold on a black silk cape inspired by the horses on the Neptune Fountain in Versailles.

The high point of this series of magnificent collections and the last to follow a theme was the Commedia dell'Arte collection in October 1938. In its way it continues February's theme, once again playing with the idea of drama and performance that was such a passion for Schiaparelli. She brought in a troupe of Pierrots, Harlequins and Columbines in chequered costumes of embroidered felt, faille and satin, mingling the influences of baroque music, Tiepolo, Picasso, Bérard and Severini, who had been obsessed with this theme since the 1920s. Three-cornered felt hats, gauze masks and accessories adorned with tinkling bells completed a collection that was the ultimate expression of Schiaparelli's style: theatricality and playfulness, individuality and irony, optical illusion and trompe l'œil.

François Lesage accompanied his father on visits to the couturière when he was very young. Half a century later, he said: 'When you look at couturiers, they may go back and use the same design elements every twenty or twenty-five years. Schiaparelli never did. For her, one good idea was the springboard to the next and she never repeated herself.' But this inexhaustible imagination still needed the right interpreter. She found this in Albert Lesage, as she herself admitted. According to François, 'If she liked something, she would say "Trrrrès bien", rolling her R's. "Vous avez trrrès bien trrrravaillé".'

Millicent Rogers in a black velvet dinner suit by Schiaparelli.
Photograph by Horst P. Horst for *Vogue*, 1938

After the break during the war years, the relationship between Lesage and Schiaparelli continued until her house closed in 1954. But it would never again be as close; she did less couture work as her perfumes became more successful. Nevertheless, their collaboration had a more decisive impact on the embroiderer's career and situation than his work with Vionnet. According to Palmer White, 'In 1927, the Lesage books had shown a turnover of 800,000 francs. For 1937, it was 1,551,539 francs.' And that financial success was coupled with an even greater asset, which today would be called their brand. Lesage's reputation grew, thanks in particular to the success of Schiaparelli's creations and the way embroidery and adornment had obviously contributed to that.

Inspired by the dynamics of this joint venture and by the international aura of the couture house, Albert considered expanding his atelier's operations, particularly by re-establishing contact with the country he had left twenty years earlier – the United States – which was a huge potential market. In a deal that was a completely new departure in the trade, he entered into an agreement with a New York embroiderer (with the very French name of

Mr Toussaint), of a kind similar to those that some fashion houses had with large American stores. He would regularly supply his partner with a seasonal set of designs aimed at transatlantic clients. He already had some idea of their tastes from his time with Marshall Field.

On 28 August 1939 Albert Lesage boarded the SS *Normandie*, the luxury liner that had been launched a few years earlier. He was travelling to New York to finalize the arrangements for a collaboration that looked promising. On 1 September, just four days after the ship set sail, Hitler invaded Poland. On 3 September, France and Britain declared war on Germany. Albert arrived in New York only to discover the impossibility of collaboration in those circumstances (and the unexpected death of Mr Toussaint). Cutting short a visit that was now pointless, he managed to return to Paris at the end of September, this time travelling on the brand-new RMS *Queen Elizabeth*.

Marie-Louise had been caught unawares by the declaration of war while she was staying at the family's second home in Mont-Dore. The family went there regularly, not just for holidays but also because the climate in the region suited Jean-Louis, who was then fifteen years old and still in poor health. When Albert returned, the family decided to take refuge in the provinces, while Albert went back to Paris on his own to try to manage the unmanageable. They found a tutor for Jean-Louis, and the twins were enrolled in a local school.

In the rue de la Grange-Batelière Albert tried to keep the business going, aided by people in the fashion business who were determined to carry on as long as possible. The Chambre Syndicale de la Haute Couture, the trade association headed by Lucien Lelong, announced that the summer collections would be shown in February 1940. The press and American buyers braved the crossing via Genoa before travelling up to Paris. They arrived in time to go to the shows, little thinking that it would be six years before they saw any more. In June 1940, France fell to Germany and people fled south. Albert had no choice but to close the atelier, leave his mother in charge of Chaville and drive across France with his sales director, Christian Powel, and a head seamstress called Olga.

above Schiaparelli, 1941

previous pages Schiaparelli, Music collection, 1937
overleaf, left Schiaparelli, 1938
overleaf, right Schiaparelli, 1937

91

Albert stayed for nine months in Mont-Dore, which escaped German occupation. Incapable of being idle, he continued to work on projects and motifs with Marie-Louise in the hope, soon dashed, that things would quickly return to normal. As well as the political upheaval, there were problems in the family. The war had created a shortage of healthcare and medicine, and Jean-Louis's health had deteriorated. He had to be sent to a sanatorium in Crans-Montana in the Swiss canton of Valais, while his maternal grandparents, brother and sister moved to Thonon-les-Bains to be close to him. In March 1941, Albert could stand it no longer and decided to return to Paris with his two assistants and reopen the atelier. He approached the fashion houses that, under the encouragement of Lucien Lelong, were trying to carry on: Schiaparelli of

above left   Albert and François Lesage, 1942
above right   Albert Lesage with his children, François and Christiane, 1941

previous pages   Worth, 1948

course, Robert Piguet, Jacques Fath, who had just moved into his new salon, and Cristóbal Balenciaga, who at that very moment, perhaps at Schiaparelli's instigation, was starting to use embroidery and passementerie on his creations.

But it was not enough for Albert to receive orders; he had to be able to fulfil them. He took on two embroiderers, but the effects of rationing and the shortages of material were already making themselves felt. He could initially use the stock inherited from Michonet and what was left from his boom period. However, he soon had to make do with whatever was available, as Palmer White writes: 'Real silk had to be replaced by rayon, when that could be obtained. Even thread was difficult to find, and he had to slip a louis d'or to a manufacturer of gold thread if he wished to receive any. Sequins were out of the question: there were no oxen available to provide the gall from which to make the gelatine... There was very little chiffon, taffeta, satin or even rayon, while velvet was hoarded like gold... Albert exercised his ingenuity by adapting embroidery to natural substances: animal and vegetable fibres, straw from cereal grasses, raffia from palm trees, flax from herbs. He even had pieces done with the jute used for potato sacks. Since yarn for embroidery came to be lacking, he resorted to cord, even string.'

It has often been said that Parisian women turned their stylishness, even when it was only improvised – wooden clogs, rubber soles cut from tyres, stocking seams drawn on bare legs – into an expression of defiance against the occupying forces. Fashion became a low-key means of resistance. A piece that Lesage created for Schiaparelli in 1942 depicts a silk carriage as black as a night under the curfew, highlighted with a few strokes of gold and fuchsia pink; the carriage window reveals what Palmer White calls 'sweethearts kissing openly to defy the Nazis in the name of love'. Making a virtue out of necessity and coming to terms with the shortage of chemical dyes, the fashion trade was forced to embrace the monochrome: jet beads, passementerie trims and frogging in monochrome black, and fabrics that were often heavy and rough (it was the memory of these austere styles that Dior was, by his own admission, trying to exorcise in his legendary collection of February 1947).

In his efforts to keep the atelier going (he also lived and had his office there), Albert cycled once a fortnight to Chaville, where his mother still lived, and stayed away from the family for over a year. When he saw Marie-Louise and the twins again, it was under tragic circumstances. In June 1942, Jean-Louis died of meningitis and tuberculosis. Albert was able to cross the unoccupied zone to be with his family. However, he had to return to rue de la Grange-Batelière after only two weeks. It was not until two years later that his family was reunited after the liberation.

In Paris, the occupying forces were putting increasing pressure on the fashion industry. In the first few years of the occupation, Lelong's strategy of keeping the fashion houses united in the capital was successful in averting the threat of closure, but as the Allies advanced and shortages increased, the situation became more difficult. Even so, designers and their suppliers found ingenious solutions. Society life continued in Paris, taking advantage of black market revenue and the shameless exploitation of the conflict by the nouveaux riches.

However, in January 1944, the Germans ordered Grès to close down, claiming that the designer's signature draped garments exceeded restrictions on the amounts of fabric allowed (although she reopened later that year with her now infamous collection in the patriotic colours of the French flag). The same happened to Balenciaga, who had been under surveillance for some time. Only a few fashion houses that had shown a more flexible attitude to the occupying forces (Marcel Rochas, Maggy Rouff, Jacques Fath) remained unconcerned. By May 1944, the stalling tactics by Lelong and the Chambre de la Haute Couture no longer worked. All Paris fashion houses were ordered to close within eight weeks. It must be one of the least known and most decisive consequences of D-Day that French Haute Couture was saved from a disastrous diktat at the eleventh hour.

The euphoria of the liberation soon faded. Shortages continued, ersatz goods were all that were available, materials were still of a poor quality, silks and furs were unobtainable, and the amount of fabric that could be used was still restricted. Hence the hostile reactions to the extravagant 'New Look', recorded in a famous photograph of housewives furiously tearing at a model's dress during a fashion shoot. In those circumstances, it was all the more essential to revive traditional French elegance and the central role of Paris. The 'Théâtre de la Mode' exhibition that opened at the Musée des Arts Décoratifs in March 1945 was perhaps the most notable evidence of that ambition.

Reviving the concept of the 18th-century fashion mannequins that allowed the latest Paris gowns to be displayed in
miniature in all the courts of Europe, the Chambre Syndicale de la
Haute Couture asked 40 couturiers, 36 dressmakers and 20 hair-
dressers to dress nearly 200 doll-like figurines with plaster faces
and wire bodies in original designs that typified French fashion.
Directed by Christian Bérard, with scenery by Cocteau, Louis
Touchagues, Emilio Terry and others, the little theatre travelled
round Europe and the United States for two years, highlighting
the skills and excellence of the French ateliers with the idea of win-
ning back foreign clients and bringing them back to Paris.
Although Lesage was not mentioned in the exhibition catalogue,
which focused mainly on designers, the Maison Lesage's work
certainly featured unobtrusively on some of the creations by his
regular clients, Lelong, Grès, Schiaparelli and Balenciaga.

Albert Lesage, facing a crisis as serious as the one he had
gone through in 1931, looked for a new source of revenue. He
found it, paradoxically, in textiles, a field in which he had been
unsuccessful fifteen years earlier. Admittedly, this time he had the
help of one of Lyon's leading silk makers, who was trying to gain
entry into the world of Haute Couture. Jean Barrioz, president of
the textile trade association in Lyon, asked Lesage to act as his
agent in Paris, to show and promote his silks to the designers he
knew. Albert accepted immediately. While acting as artistic and
technical adviser to Barrioz, Albert, still seeking new outlets, urged
him to look into artificial textiles made from cellulose acetate, a
synthetic fibre first invented in 1865 for which some firms were
developing new uses. It was in response to another campaign to
promote acetate that Line Vautrin developed the material she
called Talosel, from which she made jewelry, mirrors and objects
that are much sought after today.

Albert's entry into the textile market allowed him both to
expand his supply and to compensate for the fall in orders and the
shortage of embroidery materials. As well as Schiaparelli's unfail-
ing support, he was now receiving orders from Balenciaga, whose
career was really taking off at the time, and from a newcomer
trained by Edward Molyneux and Lucien Lelong, Pierre Balmain,

previous pages Schiaparelli, 1952

who opened his fashion house with his mother's help in 1945. Balmain had trained as an architect and his style was highly structured, often described as 'sombre and sober'. Even so, he was not averse to trimmings, decoration and ornamentation in the grand French tradition.

The sensation of 12 February 1947 and the cultivated reputation of Christian Dior retrospectively overshadowed Balmain's achievements, but in fact he enjoyed dazzling success from the start. This continued up to the 1980s, when he dressed many French and foreign stars: Danielle Darrieux, Brigitte Bardot, Michèle Morgan, Rita Hayworth, Sophia Loren and Lana Turner. He found that Albert and later Albert's successor understood and interpreted his requirements perfectly.

It was a number of years before the names Dior and Lesage were linked, when François was in charge of the firm. For embroidery Christian Dior had decided to use Lelong's old supplier, René Bégué (1887–1987), known as Rébé. Rébé remained a staunch competitor to Lesage until his firm closed in 1966, and later expressed regret that he was 100 years old and had missed what could have been a wonderful professional friendship. The two had different approaches: Rébé's, according to Palmer White, was based on the use of traditional techniques to create effects; he layered materials or combined them in unusual ways (gold braid with bugle beads, diamonds with sequins) that often gave his embroidery a density, a texture, an opulence, whereas Lesage's work was more understated.

Of their three children, Marie-Louise and Albert saw their eldest as the natural successor to take over when the time came. Jean-Louis was a cultured and sophisticated aesthete, very similar in personality to his grandmother Berthe who had looked after him during his teenage years and especially when he was in the sanatorium. However, his premature death put an end to that ambition. By chance or necessity, it turned out that one of the twins, François, had followed in the family tradition, showing an aptitude for drawing, painting and watercolours at an early age. Although Marie-Louise was modest and reserved, she nonetheless wanted her children to be free and she decided not to give them a traditional education. She enrolled them at a Montessori school where the teaching was progressive, open to the world, focused on sensory perception. Instead of games and toys, she gave them art books to familiarize them with the subject she viewed as the fabric of existence.

above François Lesage, Los Angeles, 1948

previous pages Balmain, 1956–1957

Their lives were not arid, dull or restricted. According to her grandson Jean-François, although Marie-Louise was strict and protective, she was ready to take time and adapt to the needs and development of the twins. Furthermore, the years spent in Mont-Dore and Thonon-les-Bains due to circumstances and the war allowed Christiane and François to live close to nature, to become familiar with its cycles and shapes, making a deep impression on the imagination of the future embroiderer.

'When François was nine,' writes Palmer White, 'his parents sent him to take lessons from an artist in Versailles. Here, from reproductions of drawings – by Leonardo or Michelangelo, say – and of sculpture he learned to mould plaster casts. On Thursdays, the day that schoolchildren then had off in France, he drove to Paris with his father, who dropped him on rue Fontaine to see his grandmother Lesage. After lunching with her, he would walk down to rue Grange. Ceremoniously, he went from atelier to atelier greeting everyone individually like the little gentleman he was, stopped to observe the embroideresses at work, took a look at what the draughtsmen were doing, then spread out his materials on whatever long table happened to be available and sketched.'

So François, as his son explains, found himself in the business without realizing it. When he was not at Saint-Jean de Béthune, a private school in Versailles that he attended after returning to Paris in September 1945 (and where Jean-François would also go), he spent more and more time at the atelier, which was thriving once again and had twenty-five employees. He was already designing embroidery motifs, producing swatches, and regularly accompanying his father to call on the most important clients, including Schiaparelli of course, and Balenciaga, but also the 'new wave', Pierre Balmain, Jacques Fath, Jacques Heim and Jacques Griffe. By the time he was seventeen, in 1946, his parents trusted him enough to let him oversee the teams while they visited the south. His success in the school leaving exam in June that year was the final step before he joined the firm permanently. From then on, he took an interest in all aspects of the Maison's work, not just the aesthetic and creative side, but also the accounts (which he always kept in good order), dealings with suppliers, and visits from representatives of the textile houses.

Although still suffering from wartime shortages, the firm was rapidly expanding and needed to find a way to make use of its new asset. And what better way for Albert to do this than by opening up to other countries, including the America that he had left behind twenty-five years earlier? In the Lesage family, a sense of aesthetics always seemed to be coupled with a love of travel, as we shall see again later. This was a costly and risky venture at the time, so François combined his task of representing the firm and seeking out new partners with another assignment as a diamond broker on behalf of a family friend, Edouard Sirakian.

above   Marlene Dietrich on the set of *A Foreign Affair*, 1948

previous pages   Balenciaga, 1957

On 9 November 1946, François boarded 'an old collier flying a Honduras flag and manned by a Greek crew'. The crossing on the *Myriam* was rough to say the least. Scheduled to take nine days, it actually took seventeen: 'First they were pounded by storms which lasted nearly a fortnight and attained such violence that the passengers had to be strapped to their berths and went without sleep for almost three days. At one point the cargo-less *Myriam* listed to 37 degrees in the raging seas – "a boogie-woogie dance", François later reported home.' Diverted to Baltimore because of a strike – the final ordeal after the hazardous crossing – François went to Philadelphia and then New York (and its diamond district), before crossing the United States from east to west, from Cleveland to Chicago, then from Saint Louis to Denver, seeking out contacts for one or other of his assignments. Finally, he went from Salt Lake City to Los Angeles to meet Simone Bouvet de Lozier, who had moved to the west coast from New York a few years earlier.

She acted as a mentor to François as she had to Albert, introducing him to her friends and acquaintances in Los Angeles and to many of the French community in Hollywood, of which Charles Boyer was the leading light. Keen to improve his knowledge of a language and culture about which he knew very little, François moved into a shared apartment for what he thought would be a short period, attended evening classes at UCLA, enrolled for lectures at Los Angeles City College and went to NBC radio shows on Saturday evenings to familiarize himself with the spoken language. Nevertheless, he did not neglect his dual objectives. Curiously, his work as a precious stones broker proved relatively unsuccessful. The deals he made on his various visits were unsuccessful or disappointing. Although he found that the two countries had different tastes, it was embroidery that opened up potential new markets.

Among the French expatriates whom Simone Bouvet de Lozier introduced to François was Jean Louis Berthault, who had become one of the most famous couturiers in Hollywood, known simply as Jean Louis. As a costume designer for Columbia Pictures, best known for the long black silk sheath dress worn by Rita

Hayworth in *Gilda*, Jean Louis combined his professional work with a private business dressing celebrities (for instance, he designed the sparkling flesh-toned gown worn by Marilyn Monroe when she sang for JFK in 1962). It was only natural for him to use embroidery from one of the most famous Paris ateliers in his creations. So François was asked to obtain a set of swatches from the rue de la Grange-Batelière. Encouraged by this initial success, he started approaching costume designers at the other studios, Adrian, Edith Head, Irene and Orry-Kelly, who were also Hollywood legends. They were interested, and through them he came into contact with the biggest stars of the period, Gene Tierney, Claudette Colbert, Olivia de Havilland and Lana Turner, for whom he designed several ensembles. 'I was cute, a little bit "zazou", I was a good designer, I knew the business,' he told *Le Monde* in 2009. 'I dressed Lana Turner, Ava Gardner. I knew exactly where to put the embroidery on Marlene Dietrich, where it was supposed to go.'

So he seemed to be achieving the aim of his trip when an unexpected obstacle arose, in the form of prohibitive customs duties between France and the United States, which made it impossible to sell Parisian embroidery there. The only solution was to have prototypes and designs sent to him by Albert made up in the United States. Once again, he had to find suitable workers. And once again, a chance encounter, with a young Cuban embroiderer called Elsa Diaz who already ran a small atelier, was to prove providential. They came to an agreement, then found a suitable site, an incongruous wooden building on Sunset Boulevard, which they decorated with the help of the French chamber of commerce in Los Angeles. Working for film studios, designers and private clients, the atelier had a promising start. It soon needed as many as ten embroiderers to keep up with the orders. When the studios announced that they were making several epics and large quantities of costumes were required, François was looking forward to the future with confidence and the development of the American atelier. He was even considering extending his stay to deal with the situation when a letter from Paris cast doubt on the whole project.

The letter was from his uncle, Louis Favot, telling François that his father's health was giving cause for concern. For the past few months Albert had had serious heart problems and he needed complete rest. Handing over the management of the Sunset Boulevard atelier to Elsa Diaz and Simone Bouvet de Lozier, François left immediately for New York, where he boarded the first available ship, a troop transport ship. He did not meet his uncle in Le Havre until the end of June, only to find that he had arrived two weeks too late.

Marie-Louise had immediately taken over control of the firm and she had her work cut out. Albert's death had opened up a vacuum and competitors, especially Rébé, were already snapping at their heels. Because of the successful collaboration on textiles with the Lyon silk makers, the business had to some extent moved away from embroidery. Although a few new names, Jacques Heim, Jean Dessès and Carven, had been added to the client list, other longstanding clients – Lelong, Piguet, Callot, Rochas – had left. Marie-Louise could depend on Jacques Fath, Balmain and Balenciaga as faithful customers, but she was primarily reliant on the resolve of François, the appointed heir. Despite his early experience, he still had a lot to learn. He knew only about certain aspects of the trade. He had a limited knowledge of the process of embroidery. He had never followed the production of a whole piece, from the preparation of a design to its execution, from the discussions with designers to the final application onto the garment.

Although he had accompanied his father on visits to some of the couturiers, he did not really know the business and rituals of the fashion world, which had been given a new impetus by the triumphant arrival of the New Look in 1947. The fifteen years or so that followed the war were a whirlwind of parties and dances, public or private, improvised or extravagant, rivalling in their originality and inventiveness the soirées, masquerades and garden parties of earlier times. They were both an expression of relief – a celebration of the return to life after the horrors of war – and the last glimmers of a society whose customs and way of life dated back to the beginning of the century and would be swept away in the 1960s.

With its conjunction of extraordinary talents, this was also the golden age of Parisian Haute Couture. François knew Schiaparelli well from visiting with Albert. She was still working hard, coming up with the most extraordinary flights of fancy. She had a profound influence on his career, impressing on him the need to experiment, to take risks. It was thanks to her, writes Palmer White, that François 'put the idea of developing themes for embroidery collections into his mind. With her he also became involved in the search for unusual, unexpected and amusing effects and objects.' The

page 114   Balenciaga, 1956
page 116   Balenciaga, 1959
page 117   Grace Kelly wearing Balenciaga, photographed with Prince Rainier III, 1959

Lesage atelier spent one winter eating mussels because Schiaparelli wanted to use the shells in her work. History – and especially the history of fashion – is a process of constant renewal. The atelier went through the same ordeal a few decades later when Christian Lacroix did the same thing as a witty homage.

In addition, François was able to continue and deepen his relationship with the firm's other special client, Cristóbal Balenciaga, who also encouraged him to innovate. The black of the pendants and jet beads contrasting with the blood red of a blouse or embroidered arabesques were a natural complement to the tight-fitting Spanish-style boleros and jackets. Through Balenciaga, says Palmer White, 'François learned how to use Chantilly lace in embroidery and apply it to satin, to do baroque edgings, and to design pieces that resembled Cordoba leather', materials and processes that were used again after a thirty-year interval in his collaboration with Christian Lacroix. As well as traditional materials, he introduced innovations. His experimentation with cellulose acetate derivatives, such as rhodoid, has already been mentioned in the context of his work with Jean Barrioz. Rhodoid is a hard, transparent, shiny plastic that can be dyed various colours. François had the idea of combining it with black chenille for a contrast of textures, highlighting the fluffiness of the chenille with the sharp-edged strips of rhodoid; he followed this with 'cabochons, triangles in relief and *pastilles* (pellets) enclosed by a chiffon made of cigalene, a crinkled nylon gauze which soon became all the rage.'

But the hero of the hour was of course Christian Dior, who in the ten years of his brief career managed to continue the stunning success of the New Look with a series of 'lines' in a very distinctive style. He also showed remarkable business sense, for instance creating perfumes and accessories. François eventually managed to breach the defensive wall put up around Dior by his competitor, Rébé, and offer Dior embroidery that was less opulent, more stylized than that of his competitor, especially for the summer collections in lighter and more fluid fabrics than the winter collections. Lesage's collaboration with the couturier came to an

end when Dior died suddenly, but he went on to establish an even closer relationship with Dior's successor, Yves Saint Laurent.

Described as a 'comet', Jacques Fath also had his career brought to a premature end when he died of leukemia in 1954. Dior's brilliance retrospectively overshadowed Fath's career and obscured his significance. Fath's style was less formal than that of the older man, younger and freer. It was typified by the youthful femininity of Brigitte Bardot, who wore several of his creations, and embodied in his mischievous favourite models, Lucky and Bettina. As commercially astute as Dior, his role model, Fath differed from him in the fluidity and fullness of his creations, accentuated by the way he draped yards of material directly onto the mannequins' bodies.

Fath's aim was to project a youthful and fresh image, and throughout his career he focused on the idea of 'young girls in flower', with floral motifs. In 1950 he showed a Lily collection, and his 1953 collection was on a plant theme. François Lesage was allowed free rein, creating for him sprigs of fern in coloured glass beads and horsehair foliage embroidered on a tulle ground. White writes that for one of the extravagant balls that Fath attended with his wife Geneviève, François designed an ephemeral dress incorporating fresh asparagus stalks, secured between two layers of nylon netting and scattered with rhinestones. It had to be sprayed with water every two hours to keep the plants fresh.

Pierre Balmain, another client at the time, also favoured floral motifs, but his were full of historical references and, like his palette of muted colours, straw yellow and sage green, beige and mother-of-pearl, dusky rose and silver, harked back to the stylized blooms of the 18th century. This was even reflected in the names of his creations, 'Versailles' and 'Zaïde'. Trained at Molyneux and Lelong, where he worked with Dior, Balmain escaped the fate of premature death. He continued to run his house until his death in 1982, making him one of Lesage's most faithful clients for nearly forty years.

Balmain is inseparable from 'Jolie Madame', the name of his famous perfume created in 1949 and also used as the theme of his 1952 collection. Mingling references to Jean Pillement's

previous pages   Balmain Fall/Winter 1958–1959

page 120   Lesage creation, Fall/Winter 1958–1959

fantastical designs and the scattered floral motifs of 18th-century waistcoats in embroidered lace, François made the signature gown in the collection a dazzling show of virtuosity, a masterpiece of ingenuity. He then outdid it six years later in another signature dress, simply entitled 'Paris', which combined traditional materials such as rococo ribbons with others that were totally modern, such as straw beads, hammered sequins and silk roses in faded Judith Barbier colours.

François worked for other clients who were well known at the time and are now forgotten, such as Jacques Griffe and Jean Dessès, for whom he brought back the shadowed technique that Vionnet had favoured and studded a magnificent dress with iridescent soufflé pearls. He also started working with a designer of his own age, Hubert de Givenchy, whom he had met a few years earlier at Schiaparelli's. Givenchy opened his own couture house in 1952, with Balenciaga as his mentor. François Lesage did not know that his relationship with Givenchy would last even longer than his collaboration with Pierre Balmain, ending only when Givenchy retired in 1995.

L esage continued to work with Balenciaga, Balmain and Givenchy in the decade after Dior's death, a period in which the fashion world and its values were being fundamentally redefined. Factors such as the dynamic of reconstruction, the rise of the middle class, urbanization, standardization, the rise of female emancipation and the different pace of life led to the establishment of a new kind of fashion, more accessible and less formal than Haute Couture. This was the height of the futurist utopia, the celebration of progress and new technology. In the spirit of the age, designers tried to create fashion that was more dynamic, casual, simple, easy to wear and (essentially) youthful.

There was no room, you might think, for the detailed refinement of Lesage's work in the monochrome clothes of Courrèges, Pierre Cardin's optical effects or Paco Rabanne's futuristic armour. But after the initial shock, Lesage's designer friends were adaptable (in any case, Balenciaga and Balmain were never averse to understatement and pared-down style). Although they kept up with the times, they did not lose their love of rich and opulent fabrics, of those extra touches characteristic of Haute Couture.

As we have seen, innovation and modernity had always been a hallmark of the Lesages (for instance, in the use of cellulose acetate some years earlier), and in that period they introduced and experimented with new materials, as François explained at the time in a rare description of his philosophy: 'The art of traditional embroidery', he wrote, 'consists of employing the same techniques and the same classical materials for the various styles of drawing. The very essence of embroidery for Haute Couture is to associate techniques and materials that we are not used to seeing combined. That is the secret of creating. New textiles cannot be developed by weaving wool on silk looms, or silk on wool looms. Embroidery is renewed by introducing all kinds of elements that are not predestined for embroidery. Feathers, furs, shells, leather, wool meshes, rock crystals: they can all be integrated now. Our sequins, instead of being positioned one by one, can be pushed into place in packets. To obtain reliefs, bugle beads can be arranged so as to lend depth.... What matters is creating a new and always unexpected effect and carrying it out perfectly. Unlike a machine, the hand knows no limits.'

Palmer White went on to record the results of that philosophy: 'silk, particularly for the summer, with echoes of painted wallpaper and sophisticated country scenes, applications of chiffon on tulle, cotton organdy embroidered with point lace and matt gold ... an effect of weaving through a play of materials, the mingling of silk thread with straw or cellophane chenille.' The ever resourceful François also explored the theme of gardens seen

opposite   Balmain, 1955

previous pages   Balenciaga, 1960

above   Cristóbal Balenciaga, 1927

overleaf, left   Balenciaga, 1967
overleaf, right   Balenciaga, 1961

through Venetian blinds, braids woven from cellophane ribbon, feather embroidery protected beneath a layer of tulle; he created 'backgrounds filled in with fanciful sequins, little flowers, clover leaves, stars, plastic squares, cabochons, Scottish plaids, and plastic feathers.' Those were just the initial results of the exciting capacity for innovation that would always be associated with the name of François Lesage, a worthy heir to the family tradition, and was the secret of his success.

The couture house opened by Yves Saint Laurent after his time with Dior also marked a turning point and coincided with the arrival of new Haute Couture designers of a similar generation to François: Emanuel Ungaro and Jean-Louis Scherrer at their respective fashion houses, Marc Bohan at Dior, Michel Goma at Patou and Jules-François Crahay at Lanvin. They would work in partnership with Lesage throughout their careers. With the simplified lines of the period (between mini and maxi), using geometric and abstract patterns, they still clung to an idea of fashion that Balenciaga, when he closed his boutique in 1968, was one of the first to deem out of step with the times. Yves Saint Laurent would continue his magnificent work for over thirty years before coming to the same conclusion. But in the meantime, he remained one of the leading lights in the redefinition of fashion and the emergence of a new creative style.

Although Yves Saint Laurent clearly saw Haute Couture as his true métier throughout his career, it must not be forgotten that the creation of the Rive Gauche line in 1966 also made him a central figure in the advent of Prêt-à-Porter, which a few decades later offered François Lesage unlimited scope for experimentation. At first, however, the collaboration between embroiderer and couturier, which had produced some real masterpieces, always occurred within the traditions of Parisian Haute Couture. Yves

Saint Laurent initially approached Lesage because he had worked with Vionnet and Schiaparelli, who had shaped Saint Laurent's view of fashion. The dozens of rhinestone lips scattered across an evening coat in the 1971 Spring/Summer collection were an initial homage to Schiaparelli; and he paid homage to her again from time to time in his collections, for example with variations on *commedia dell'arte* motifs – as reinvented by Cocteau and Picasso – in the Fall/Winter 1979–1980 collection, the collar of a satin jacket encrusted with rhinestones and gold for Fall/Winter 1980–1981, and the cape adorned with two birds, in front of a sun with embroidered rays, from the Spring/Summer 1988 Braque collection.

In the 1970s, one of the first successful collaborations between Lesage and Yves Saint Laurent was a range of long cardigans embroidered with various motifs ('imitation Irish sweaters, houndsteeth in trompe l'œil, imitation lizard, turtle shells, crocodiles, tree bark and so on…'). Working with difficult materials to satisfy the requirements of the couturiers (Yves Saint Laurent and Marc Bohan at Dior), François used stiff materials such as leather, as well as those that were considered impossible because they were too soft and elastic, such as jersey (it had to be lined first and the lining was then removed once the embroidery was finished).

But these ventures were only the prelude to a series of Saint Laurent shows that became legendary in the history of fashion, in which Lesage showed off his extraordinary skills. The Russian collection of 1976, the Chinese collection the year after, the Diaghilev and Picasso collection in 1979, followed by those dedicated to Aragon, Apollinaire and Cocteau (1980), Matisse and Léger (1981–1982), and Braque (the bodice fronts adorned with flying birds called for enormous inventiveness). For the tribute to Aragon, Apollinaire and Cocteau, Saint Laurent scattered literary quotations in black suede picked out in rhinestones on a pink satin evening jacket, and paid tribute to the eyes of Elsa Triolet – who was married to Aragon – in rhinestones and gold accentuated with jet on a blue velvet ground. The series culminated in the 1988 'Homage to Artists' show in which the masterpieces were jackets embroidered all over with Vincent

opposite Yves Saint Laurent, Braque collection, Spring/Summer 1988 Haute Couture.
Photographed at the Yves Saint Laurent Retrospective Couture Show, January 2002, Paris

previous pages Yves Saint Laurent, Hommage à ma Maison,
Spring/Summer 1990 Haute Couture

Van Gogh's irises and sunflowers. Representing six hundred hours of work, they were reputed to be among the most expensive couture pieces in the world.

Nothing was more certain to fire François's imagination than this unlimited scope for creativity, this playful attitude to appearances. Like Saint Laurent, François Lesage loved trompe l'œil and visual puns, something he further explored when he launched a line of accessories: false shirt fronts for evening dresses, false pleats for skirts, false belts of embroidered cord. 'He also introduced another technique: motifs cut out one by one and applied to a fabric by means of new thermopasted films. From there on, this technique, derived from industry, would make possible miracles that could not have been envisaged with the old collage techniques, such as the "film Guta", a thin rubber sheet which stuck too fast and left spots. In the years to come, François was to develop this thermopasted film process in all possible forms, including real gold sheets and velvet on chiffon.'

However, François did not only produce his magnificent work for Yves Saint Laurent. The work he did for Jean-Louis Scherrer's Indian collection for the summer of 1981 rivalled that of the embroiderers of Madras (his son would later draw on their skills). He reinvented traditional cashmere motifs with gold thread and lamé appliqué on a ground embroidered with sage green sequins. As a homage to Mariano Fortuny, he suggested to Givenchy and Balmain an interpretation of the characteristic patterns of the Venetian couturier, by means of thermally fused films that he could use to apply flat areas of gold onto Fortuny's favourite fabrics: silk chiffon, panne and crushed velvet. He started working with Hanae Mori in 1980 – three years after she had opened her fashion house in Paris – creating clouds of diaphanous butterflies, which were her symbols, a pattern of snowflakes in rhinestones and silver thread on a midnight-blue satin bolero, and a long jacket embroidered all over with foliage in monochrome mauve and blue sequins on a black ground.

By the beginning of the 1980s, the atelier had expanded considerably as work picked up again. It employed a head designer, five designers, two modellers, an assistant, a production manager,

opposite   Yves Saint Laurent, 1983

page 138   Katoucha Niane models the Yves Saint Laurent Braque collection,
Spring/Summer 1988 Haute Couture. Photographed at the Yves
Saint Laurent Retrospective Couture Show, January 2002, Paris
page 139   Yves Saint Laurent, Aria collection, Spring/Summer 1988 Haute Couture

swatch-makers and embroiderers. True to his ethos, François considered his staff a second family, which sometimes took the place of his first. 'When the collections are on', he told *L'Officiel de la Mode*, 'we sleep here. Camp beds are set up. I do the cooking myself in the evening. At midday on Sunday there are forty of us at lunch.' Azzedine Alaïa later worked in the same way in his atelier on rue de Moussy. This communal living was often necessary because of the invariably urgent and last-minute demands of the designers. This is still a common fault in the industry, with fashion houses taking the attitude that work does not count unless it is urgent. The result is a dizzying process involving impossible deadlines, the forty hours it takes to make even a small swatch measuring twenty-five by twenty-five centimetres, and the need to come up with ideas that meet the couturier's requirements. 'A falling leaf, an autumn colour can suggest an idea,' François explained. 'I found the theme for the last collection when I was leafing through a newspaper at three o'clock in the morning. It all started with a camellia. The collection grew from that.' The combination of happy chance and relentless discipline defined the work of the atelier from one season to the next. This precision machinery gathered even greater pace over the years that followed.

As well as the power suit, the redefinition of femininity, clean lines and new money, the 1980s were notable for the emergence of the 'fashion for fashion', the Prêt-à-Porter lines that were booming internationally and the rise of new designers whose individuality instantly became a brand. An indirect and unexpected consequence of these changes for the Maison Lesage was a third American venture, this time a successful one. Precisely because they offered something different from their European counterparts, New York designers had become increasingly significant; in light of the achievements of Claire McCardell and others, their designs were considered simpler, more functional, better suited to the tastes of a wider clientele than Paris fashion. A historic fashion show in Versailles in 1973, which had brought together some of the big names in couture from both continents, with the aim of giving them equal status, had proved pivotal in this shift.

What might be called the pragmatic approach of American fashion may seem at odds with the extravagant use of ornamentation and sparkling embroidery. But while he was in Paris for the collections in early 1982, top US designer Calvin Klein visited the atelier on rue de la Grange-Batelière. According to François Lesage, Klein reacted to the organized chaos, the drawers overflowing with beads, bugles, embroidery and swatches, like 'a child in a pastry shop'. 'The American', writes Palmer White, 'dashed over to Paris to see more and ordered a mountain for his collection to be shown at the end of October – that is, in six weeks. Lesage et Cie worked day and night, and Mr Klein's assistant jumped on to Concorde every three days to pick up the pieces that had been finished in the interval.' Success bred success. The collection was so well received that although, according to his biographer, he was slightly intimidated, François decided to show his creations (as he had done in Los Angeles nearly four decades earlier, that time without any qualms) to the aristocracy of New York couture: Bill Blass, Geoffrey Beene and Oscar de la Renta, whom he would later meet again as head of Balmain, as well as Carolina Herrera, Mary McFadden and Carolyne Roehm. He acquired a new group of faithful customers.

The Paris couturiers were not to be outdone, and it was at that point that Lesage had a critical encounter with one of the leading figures in the fashion world, Karl Lagerfeld, already known for his anachronistic ponytail, whose move to Chanel and change of status were making the headlines. His arrival on the scene would have an unexpected and dramatic effect on the Lesage fortunes.

In the worlds of Haute Couture and in particular Prêt-à-Porter, designers were emulating and challenging each other in uninhibited competition. From Klimt to Kandinsky, from insect wings to tribal motifs or a beach strewn with debris (which he made for Thierry Mugler), François, like the jeweler Robert Goossens,

opposite Detail of a jacket designed by Karl Lagerfeld for Simone Veil, worn on her election to the Académie Française, 2010

previous pages Lesage school, 1996

found the most varied and unusual sources of inspiration. According to a report in *Le Monde*, 'One day Yves Saint Laurent phoned him. "Come and see!" He rushed over. Saint Laurent showed him the reflection of the crystal chandelier and the Paris sky in the Lalanne mirrors and told him, "That's what I want". Lesage came back with three versions, in morning, noon and evening light. Saint Laurent exclaimed, "That's wonderful! We'll make them all." It took 350 hours to embroider each piece.'

This was a time of excess (the 11,000 hours of work and the million dollars spent on the decoration of a cape, dress and train for the wife of an African ruler appointing himself emperor in 1977 were just one example). Above all, it was a time when Haute Couture went through a period of upheaval (according to Palmer White, turnover rose by 25 per cent between 1980 and 1981), and Christian Lacroix burst onto the scene in an explosion of shapes and colours. The young designer immediately established a good relationship with François, so much so that Lacroix saw François as his fashion 'godfather'.

Lesage's bold style was perfectly suited to the collage effects and unexpected combinations favoured by Lacroix. In Lacroix's Spring/Summer collection for Jean Patou in 1985, there was a half-Texan, half-Camargue-style shirt in golden yellow organza embroidered with sequins, overlaid with jet hearts and mirrors. The next year brought cut-out shapes, embossed leather, shades of gold and bronze, and animal or floral motifs, all provided by François and supplemented by Lacroix's own motifs inspired by petrified wood. In the summer of 1986, a flame-coloured, hand-painted dress covered with large black scrolls was teamed with a black velvet bustier embroidered with broad spirals of matt gold, inspired by Léon Bakst. It was more than just a collaboration; the opening of Lacroix's own fashion house on 26 July 1987 sealed a friendship that would last until François's death twenty-five years later.

opposite   Christian Lacroix, 1991

overleaf   Christian Lacroix, 1988

151

Whether it was cause or effect, Lacroix's exuberant style arrived at a time when Prêt-à-Porter was starting to move closer to Haute Couture. Ready-to-Wear was becoming increasingly significant in financial terms, with a turnover of a billion francs in 1982, and was receiving more media coverage. This was the start of a ten-year period in which anything seemed possible. Designers wanted to be extravagant; they started to adorn their Ready-to-Wear lines with embroidery that, because of its cost, had formerly featured only on Haute Couture. This immediately brought in more work for the Maison Lesage, and extra staff were taken on. In order to balance the periods of intense work before the collections and the interim periods in which work now had to be found for around a hundred embroiderers, François decided to introduce a new line and a different field of experimentation, creating a range of accessories and embroidered jewelry to be sold in a small boutique in Place Vendôme (by a remarkable coincidence, the store that had previously been Schiaparelli's).

In 1985 he took on a young designer, Gérard Trémolet, who had started his career with Jean-Louis Scherrer at the age of twenty before joining an accessories firm where he was in charge of the whole production process, from design to marketing. That was obviously a major asset for Lesage. For François, it was also a way to reconnect with an earlier chapter in the Maison's history. Albert had produced jewelry and embroidered accessories for Schiaparelli in the 1930s. Under its own name, Lesage was able to sell cuffs and bracelets, necklaces and earrings, bags, stoles, shawls, belts and chains, often featuring trompe-l'œil effects, in a wide variety of materials: crystals and sequins, tiles from antique mosaics, 19th-century jet beads and rhinestones.

Imperceptibly, François Lesage had become a designer in his own right, a partner rather than a supplier to the leading couturiers. That was the decade in which he was recognized and became part of the fashion establishment. He received a number of awards: the Grand Prix des Métiers d'Art and the Medal of the City of Paris in 1984, then the Grand Prix de la Création de la Ville de Paris five years later. As a rare distinction, in 1990 the Maison became a member of the Comité Colbert, which brings together, represents and protects the leading French luxury labels. The first exhibition on the history of Lesage was put on at the Fashion Institute of Technology in New York in 1987, a year before another retrospective at the Palais Galliera that then went on to Tokyo and Los Angeles.

Making the most of this successful period, which was somewhat unstable, François invested in the future. He sought out and collected as many rare and discarded materials as he could (including sixty tonnes of beads and antique sequins) from firms that had closed or were about to close before their stocks were

opposite Fei Fei Sun models Chanel Spring/Summer 1984 Haute Couture.
Photograph by Steven Meisel for the May 2015 issue of US *Vogue*

previous pages Chanel, 1983

broken up. He organized as best he could the 50,000 swatches from the archives, including those from Michonet, piled up at rue de la Grange-Batelière. He took over Hamelin, a furnishing embroidery firm based on rue du Mail, which was to play an unexpected role in the firm's future growth. As someone who respected and admired all forms of talent, he also became involved in the business of a young Danish designer named Lars Hillingso (1938–2005), who happened to be his neighbour. Hillingso enjoyed ten successful years with his Lars Paris label, going on to design several outfits for Queen Margrethe of Denmark and her mother Queen Ingrid. François supported him with unusual generosity and regularly produced embroidery for his eveningwear.

Finally, concerned about the future of a craft that relied entirely on a steady supply of expert seamstresses, in 1992 François decided to set up a school alongside the atelier to pass on the unique skills of the embroiderers, some of whom – the 'old hands' – had been born at the very beginning of the 20th century. The school became an integral part of the Maison Lesage, building an international reputation and training both keen embroiderers and future couturiers.

Generous by nature and a grasshopper rather than an ant, François did not see the lean times coming and failed to predict the scale of the economic crisis in the late 1980s. The cumulative effects of the second oil crisis, the recession, the fall in industrial employment, the collapse of the stock exchange and of the rapidly accumulated wealth led to the sudden disappearance of clients, particularly those from the Middle East, for whom expense had previously been no object. Whether it was intuition or a symptom, it was coupled with a complete redefinition of the fashion business with the arrival of Japanese designers and the trend towards deconstruction, minimalism and grunge. There was little or no place in these austere designs for the pleasure of accessories, the sensuality of decoration, the vivid accents of embroidery. The store in Place Vendôme had to close.

François compared the 1992 crisis with the one in 1929. Although the earlier one was more serious in global terms, this new crisis was just as disastrous for the Maison Lesage. As Albert had been in the 1930s, François was faced with a sudden reversal of fortune. Despite the paternal relationship he had had with his 'family' of embroiderers, he had to lay off some of his 'girls'. With new competition from cheaper workshops in the now-international fashion trade, there was no hope of a recovery. He drew heavily on his personal savings to keep the business afloat.

While the concentration and polarization around a few luxury corporations that formed in that period has continued ever since, the role of the 'stylist' – an interpreter of trends who is supposed to capture and reflect the current mood (and take account of the demands of marketing) – has replaced that of the couturier, whose vision comes from their own imagination and changes over time. The retirement of Yves Saint Laurent in 2002 and the closure of Christian Lacroix's fashion house seven years later, as unfair and regrettable as it was premature, were the two most notable signs of that change. The future of staunchly independent companies such as Lesage, which relied on a definition of couture that was now in question, seemed uncertain at the very least. One of the leading lights of the fashion industry, Chanel, took the shrewd decision, which of course was also in its own interest, to act as a *deus ex machina* and help François out of his difficulties. The fact that Chanel also saw itself as a family firm could not be purely accidental.

above   Inès de La Fressange models Chanel Fall/Winter 1983–1984 Haute Couture

overleaf   Chanel Fall/Winter 2016–2017 Haute Couture   161

In this troubled period in the Lesage story, an unexpected and exciting new prospect was about to open up for the family.

François had had three children, Martine, Jean-Louis and Marion, with his first wife Colette Oudenot, a former designer with Jacques Griffe. With his second wife Gisela Grube von Klewitz, who designed masks for the opera, he had a son, Jean-François, born on 28 December 1965. Jean-François shared a birthday with his maternal grandmother, a Berlin aristocrat whom he admired for her quiet distinction. At an early age he showed signs of the same artistic sense as his father and grandfather and even his great-grandfather, Gustave, who had

above   Jean-François Lesage, Pondicherry, 2009

previous pages   Vastrakala atelier, Chennai, India

worked for the publishing house Hachette, dealing particularly with engravings and illustrations.

François himself was different from Albert. Although prematurely separated from his father by the circumstances explained earlier, he had a strong attachment to family. In his view, children should be free, as he had been, to find and follow their own path. He was affectionate and kind but somewhat distant, absorbed as he was in his work and what he thought of as his other 'family' at the atelier. Rather than a father, for Jean-François he was a model, a guide, a godfather, a friend, a benevolent presence.

Jean-François had been fascinated by history since he was a child. He loved to lose himself in stories and biographies, and had a special interest in historical decor and living environments. He sometimes amused himself by building reconstructions out of polystyrene. Having spent his childhood in the family home in Chaville, he then went – not all that enthusiastically, it must be said – to Saint-Jean de Béthune, the school that François had also attended. Escaping the fate that had led to François having to take over from his father, he passed his baccalauréat in the arts, then studied law and history of art at the École du Louvre. He went on to become an auctioneer, carving a profession out of an interest that had inspired regular visits to the Versailles auction house, as well as local antique dealers, from the age of sixteen.

He had always been fascinated by the culture of India, which he first visited at the age of nineteen. This trip would completely change the course of his life. He even spoke of a seminal moment when, during a blackout in Benares, he was struck by the sight of a single patch of light in the sea of darkness: it was the figure of a lone embroiderer silhouetted in his workshop, completely focused on his work, as if indifferent to everything going on around him. Jean-François told a journalist, 'After meeting Indian embroiderers in Benares in the early 1990s, I was bitten by the family bug and from then on I never wanted to do anything else.'

On a second trip, this time to Madras (now Chennai), he discovered the ancient embroidery traditions of the villages in the region. Bringing together his love of ornament, his passion for India and the famous family business, he conceived the idea of

setting up a studio using the skills of the Indian embroiderers to work on some of the Hamelin orders. For someone with a passionate interest in the history of objects and design, it seemed a natural step to revive the trade in embroidery between India and France that had existed at the end of the 18th century and even long before, from the earliest days of a technique that, according to legend, originated from Persia.

So in 1993, with his friend Patrick Savouret and two Indian partners, Malavika Shivakumar and Sandeep Rao, he went on to set up a company called Vastrakala ('the art of textiles' in Sanskrit), in a partnership that reflected the blended nature of the venture. His aim was to bring together embroiderers who until then had been scattered throughout the villages of Tamil Nadu (the state of which Chennai is the capital) and put them to work in the best possible conditions. Supplying Paris with embroidery at a cost that bore no comparison to the costs of the French ateliers, he provided his embroiderers with an income and a standard of living unparalleled in India. This ethical attitude has never left him. In an interview in 2010, he explained: 'I don't work on the basis that embroidery is French or Indian, because it is Persian. But I marry together the particular qualities of France and India to give our embroidery a special added value. France is a melting pot for experimentation, whereas India stays true to its traditions. That's why we need to think of this as a sharing of our strengths and weaknesses.'

With their needles and hooks, using age-old methods (sketching, pricking out the pattern, transfer and pouncing), embroidering between two and five square centimetres an hour, using universal techniques such as straight stitch, velvet stitch and shadow stitch, the Indian artisans produce work that is almost unbelievable, if only because of the sheer size of the areas they usually have to work on.

With the help of Jean-François and the contacts he had made professionally, they were soon working for leading designers such as Alberto Pinto, Jacques Garcia, François-Joseph Graf, Juan-Pablo Molyneux, Jacques Grange, Roberto Peregalli, Jean-Louis Deniot, Peter Marino and many others. But the thousands of hours of work that the embroiderers put in are not simply for rich

previous pages   Jeanne Lanvin's bedroom, created in 1925, now at the Musée des Arts Décoratifs, Paris. Embroidery identical to the original in collaboration with F.J. Graf

private clients. The reputation and success of the company are just as much due to prestigious public sector commissions. The firm's first project was making an identical replica of the decor of the Opéra Garnier in Monte Carlo ('we remade the pelmet of the stage curtain, the lambrequin on the royal boxes and the side boxes from an old photo in six weeks'), but the most notable example is surely a reconstruction of Jeanne Lanvin's bedroom for the Musée des Arts Décoratifs, Paris. The walls, curtains, radiators and radiator caps are all embroidered. But these are just examples of the challenges that arise every day, including work as varied as the restoration of the king's bedroom and Madame Fouquet's canopied bed in Vaux-le-Vicomte, the viceroy's state dining room in Delhi, and the furniture, tapestries and hangings in a room in Moritzburg Castle near Dresden.

At first, François was fairly sceptical and did not get involved. It seemed 'unimaginable' to him to go and live in India. But he soon recognized that the project made sense and even visited his son in Madras several times. This unexpected turn in the Lesage story came at a time when the Paris ateliers were once again starting to work for an industry that had been given a new impetus by the arrival of foreign designers such as John Galliano, Marc Jacobs and Alexander McQueen in the leading French fashion houses. But this return to business as usual was not enough to resolve all the doubts about the future of the firm and the preservation of its unique skills.

Although the focus on marketing and returns on investment must be considered one of the drawbacks of the new type of focused and globalized fashion that emerged towards the end of the 20th century, some of the players were shrewd enough to avoid direct control of this kind, banking on the long term. Reliant on the unique skills of artisans and jewelers, Chanel in particular quickly realized that some of the ateliers were in a precarious position and risked closure in the near future in the absence of successors.

The 1985 takeover of the jewelers Desrues, on the initiative of Françoise Montenay who was at the time president of Chanel, was the first of a series. Chanel decided to try to preserve the crafts that were crucial to the biggest names in fashion. At the turn of the millennium, a subsidiary was set up, significantly named Paraffection, to buy and support craft ateliers, some of which had been supplying the company since the days of Mademoiselle Chanel. Following Desrues, they gradually bought up the feather-workers Lemarié, the shoemakers Massaro, the milliners Michel, the goldsmith Goossens and many others. Under Françoise Montenay's successor Bruno Pavlovsky, who is president of Chanel's *activités mode*, the organization now encompasses around thirty firms and workshops and seems still to be open to further acquisitions.

It seemed logical for Lesage to become part of this organization, the most obvious reasons being the collaborative relationship and mutual respect that had existed between Lesage and Karl Lagerfeld since his arrival at Chanel. Lagerfeld was a central figure in the rise of Prêt-à-Porter in the 1970s, causing a sensation when he joined Chanel in 1983. At the time, the company was something of a sleeping beauty and he aimed to awaken it with his characteristic fashion sense and skill. With his witty style and veiled allusions, Lagerfeld set to work reinterpreting the world of Chanel. Starting a collaboration whose outcome neither of them could then have foreseen, he asked Lesage to work with him on the Haute Couture collections, first of all on the theme of the famous Coromandel screens that Gabrielle Chanel had collected since she was young: 'It began with Karl just like that in 1983. He told me, go and look at the Coromandels, and that was it.'

In fact, that was just the start of a series of variations on the motif. The most memorable may have been the three embroidered coats for the Haute Couture Fall/Winter collection in 1996, each of which took 800 hours to make. It was also the first of countless masterpieces and demonstrations of virtuosity. A particularly notable example was the dress embroidered with gold thread inspired by a Hindu artefact in the Spring/Summer Haute Couture show in 1996, which took nearly 2,200 hours to make.

Lagerfeld took Gabrielle Chanel's characteristic symbols – the camellia, the pearls, the quilting, the chains, the costume jewelry and even the tweed – and gave them a playful and quirky twist. He suggested to Lesage that he should reproduce them in

opposite Shalom Harlow in a dress by Karl Lagerfeld for the Chanel Spring/Summer 1996 Haute Couture collection. Photograph by Irving Penn for the April 1996 issue of US *Vogue*

previous pages Chanel Fall/Winter 1983–1984 Haute Couture

the collections in the most unlikely materials, including concrete, plastic, wood, raffia and metal. That, of course, appealed to the embroiderer's love of risk and innovation.

The baroque jewels in trompe-l'œil embroidery that adorned a magnificent dress in the first Haute Couture collection for the summer of 1983 were reinterpreted more than thirty years later for the Fall/Winter 2016–2017 collection. The quilted lozenges and gold chain strap of the Chanel handbag were mischievously transposed onto a suit embroidered with black sequins and a trompe-l'œil chain for the 1986–1987 Fall/Winter collection. The same motif was used again four years later on a more lavish creation embroidered all over with beads, before being reinterpreted as a striking 3D effect on a suit for the 2015–2016 Fall/Winter collection, now in the Metropolitan Museum of Art, New York.

An evening gown from 1997, made from an openwork trellis filled with camellias in embroidered tulle, was the most striking example of a theme that was frequently found in Lesage–Lagerfeld collaborations, in many different versions and in a sometimes very stylized form, embroidered with beads, sequins or chains. But the references to Chanel, who also inspired the mosaic patterns in the 2010 Paris–Byzance collection and the starry motifs for the 2013–2014 Paris–Dallas collection, were not Lagerfeld's only source of inspiration. Over the years, François Lesage was asked to rework motifs from Kandinsky (in 1986 and 1998), Malevich (2002) and Popova (2008), along with others from the 18th century, which was one of the couturier's favourite sources of inspiration, from the matt whiteness of Sèvres porcelain (Spring/Summer 1985 Haute Couture collection) to the pastel tones of Watteau and a gleaming casket in mother-of-pearl. Virginie Viard, who joined Chanel in 1987, became artistic director of the fashion collections in 2019, but took her first steps at the House's design studio overseeing the embroidery for the Haute Couture collection, building a close relationship with the designer and with François Lesage.

In 2002, the Maison Lesage was invited to join Paraffection. This was both a logical consequence of the long collaboration with Chanel and an ideal solution to the problem of keeping the House going and safeguarding the future of François's 'family', the development of the school and all the avenues for passing down the skills he had championed for so many years. Of course he would no longer be fully in charge; he would lose some of the control he had always guarded so jealously. But it was a small sacrifice to make, because Chanel had been shrewd enough to grant creative freedom to the other ateliers and those who had forged their identities, even after they became part of Paraffection. That strengthened François's relationship with Karl Lagerfeld, even though he was not obliged to work exclusively with Chanel. The aim of the new subsidiary was specifically to ensure the survival of the chosen ateliers in all aspects of their work, while also allowing them to continue working with their regular clients and take on new commissions.

So in the last decade of his life, François did not have to worry about survival or the cares of day-to-day management. He was able to focus on his real passion, his creative work, both for familiar clients, such as Valentino, John Galliano at Dior and Marc Jacobs at Vuitton, and for designers just starting out in their careers like Alexandre Vauthier, Jason Wu and L'Wren Scott.

François died on 1 December 2011 and did not live to see the impressively direct translation of this dialogue between the old and the new, between two stages in the story of the Maison Lesage, in the collection of eighteen designs by Christian Lacroix for Schiaparelli in July 2013. It was a symbolic opportunity for the atelier to come full circle, to give meaning to the dialogue between two dynamically creative worlds working in harmony, and to surpass itself via the jet frogging on a blood red bolero or a jeweled lobster with beaded shell and antennae.

opposite *The Coromandel dress IV* by Cathleen Naundorf, 2016.
Chanel Fall/Winter 1996–1997 Haute Couture

overleaf, left *Coco on travel – The Japanese garden XIV* by Cathleen Naundorf, 2016.
Chanel Fall/Winter 2014–2015 Haute Couture
overleaf, right *Coco on travel – The Japanese garden XI* by Cathleen Naundorf, 2016.
Chanel Fall/Winter 2014–2015 Haute Couture

Of course the membership of a large group, the wish to develop and promote the label, the need to seek out new customers and satisfy their demands were not without consequences. Soon after Chanel bought Lesage, it became clear that the building on rue de la Grange-Batelière was now too small and impractical to be fit for purpose. In an understandable desire to reorganize and save money, the company decided to move most of the craft ateliers under the Paraffection umbrella to a single set of premises that were spacious and functional.

So the Lesage atelier and archive went to join those of Lemarié, Massaro, Maison Michel and Goossens on an old industrial site of several thousand square metres on the banks of the Canal de l'Ourcq in Pantin, then in the early stages of the transformation that has made it a major hub for the fashion industry. This decision did not, however, mean giving up the five-storey

building on rue de la Grange-Batelière that was an integral part of the Lesage identity. The plan was to expand the school, which was receiving more and more applications, and a little later use the building for the Paris offices of Jean-François's firm, which had also become part of Chanel's Métiers d'Art group under the name Lesage Intérieurs.

The new premises were less attractive, but larger and more efficient. Eighty tonnes of furniture and fittings and over 75,000 embroidery swatches were transported in 2012 from the labyrinth of little rooms in the 9th arrondissement to the bright and functional, if somewhat sterile, spaces of the northern suburbs.

Murielle Lemoine had joined Lesage on the recommendation of a friend thirty years earlier and had been there ever since, first as purchasing manager and then working alongside François on Prêt-à-Porter client relations. She was witness to a change of which François had only seen the start. The crisis in the early 1990s, coupled with the first Gulf War, caused total upheaval in the trade and in the very definition of fashion. That led to a drastic reduction in the number of Haute Couture clients and the exponential growth of Prêt-à-Porter, which changed in its turn, moving closer and closer to the sophistication of couture. This growth actually reversed the process that had started in the 1970s. Like the butterfly effect, the move to Pantin was really only a distant consequence of these changes, as was the closure of many ateliers and suppliers (Lesage's alone were reduced from nearly 500 to little more than 100 in the space of around thirty years).

François thought of another solution to the problem and the drop in Haute Couture embroidery clients. Like Albert before him, he would turn to the textile industry to explore new potential. He decided to try something different, at first with his somewhat empirical response to Karl Lagerfeld's wish to 'reinvent' Chanel's famous tweeds. The earliest experiments, woven by an atelier he had approached, bore more resemblance to a floor cloth than anything else, a name that stuck ironically to that form of experimental tweed. François then approached Maria Messner, who specialized in that kind of weaving and claimed to be able to 'weave the impossible'. Her firm in south-west France, ACT 3 (standing

opposite   Chanel Spring/Summer 2016 Haute Couture

page 182   Chanel Spring/Summer 2017 Ready-to-Wear
pages 184–185   Gigi Hadid with Karl Lagerfeld during fittings
for the Chanel Spring/Summer 2016 Haute Couture collection

above   Hubert Barrère, 2018

page 188   Vittoria Ceretti models 'Diane' tweed, Chanel 2017–2018 Cruise 'Greece'
page 189   Chanel 2013 Cruise 'Versailles'
page 190   Chanel Spring/Summer 2013 Ready-to-Wear
page 191   Chanel Spring/Summer 2014 Ready-to-Wear

for Association Création Tissage 3), set up in 1996, had worked a lot with Christian Lacroix and, as its slogan indicated, it did not shrink from any challenge. Colour, textures, materials: everything was included in the quest for innovation and originality. A deconstructed and frayed 'floor cloth tweed' made of the most varied and unexpected materials (even zip fasteners and nylon thread) for subsequent collections evolved from Lagerfeld's original desire to move away from the traditional use and image of tweed, literally by unpicking it.

These experiments led to a completely new creative field for Lesage. The work on tweeds opened up a range of possibilities and a dedicated department was even set up in the ateliers. As was the firm's usual policy, and that of the Métiers d'Art generally, besides the two designers working exclusively for Chanel, a team was also created to meet the needs of other designers and one-off orders.

Another person involved in the reinvention of Lesage was Hubert Barrère. He and François had crossed paths many times. Always a dreamer, the young Hubert spent his childhood reading and drawing, fascinated by the world of fashion. However, he was forced to put his dreams aside and study law to satisfy his family's wishes. But a passion so deep could not be ignored forever. Leaving his studies behind him, to the displeasure of his parents, he decided to enrol at the École de la Chambre Syndicale de la Couture Parisienne and train to become a designer. Despite this choice meaning that he had to live by his wits and take on any minor jobs he could get, the hardship was nothing in comparison to the joy of following his true calling, which eventually led him to meet François.

Although he had worked with Lesage's competitors, the two men had a good relationship, getting together regularly to eat and talk. Barrère's admiration for François Lesage and his firm, his concern to preserve his heritage, the collaboration with Karl Lagerfeld and Virginie Viard, then the head of the studio, dating back to 1997 and the knowledge of historical embroidery in Chanel's creations, led him to accept Paraffection's offer and he was appointed as artistic director of the House, with particular responsibility for managing Lesage's relationship with Chanel, whose eight collections a year required no fewer than 50 to 100 swatches.

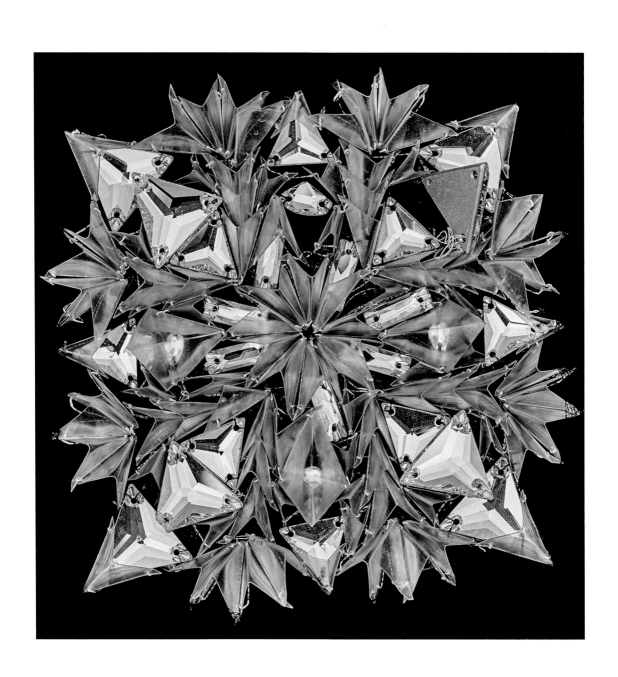

above   Dalila Betka and Véronique Barbier in the Lesage atelier in Pantin, 2018

pages 194–195   Chanel Fall/Winter 2013–2014 Haute Couture
page 196   Chanel Fall/Winter 2015–2016 Haute Couture
198   *page 197*   Ondria Hardin models Chanel Fall/Winter 2015–2016 Haute Couture

above   Margot Perotin (left) and Caroline Maréchal (right) in the Lesage atelier in Pantin, 2018

overleaf, left   Chanel 2018–2019 'Paris–New York' Métiers d'Art
overleaf, right   Chanel Fall/Winter 2013–2014 Haute Couture
pages 202–203   Chanel Fall/Winter 2013–2014 Haute Couture
page 204   Dior Fall/Winter 2017–2018 Haute Couture
page 205   Valentino Spring/Summer 2014 Haute Couture

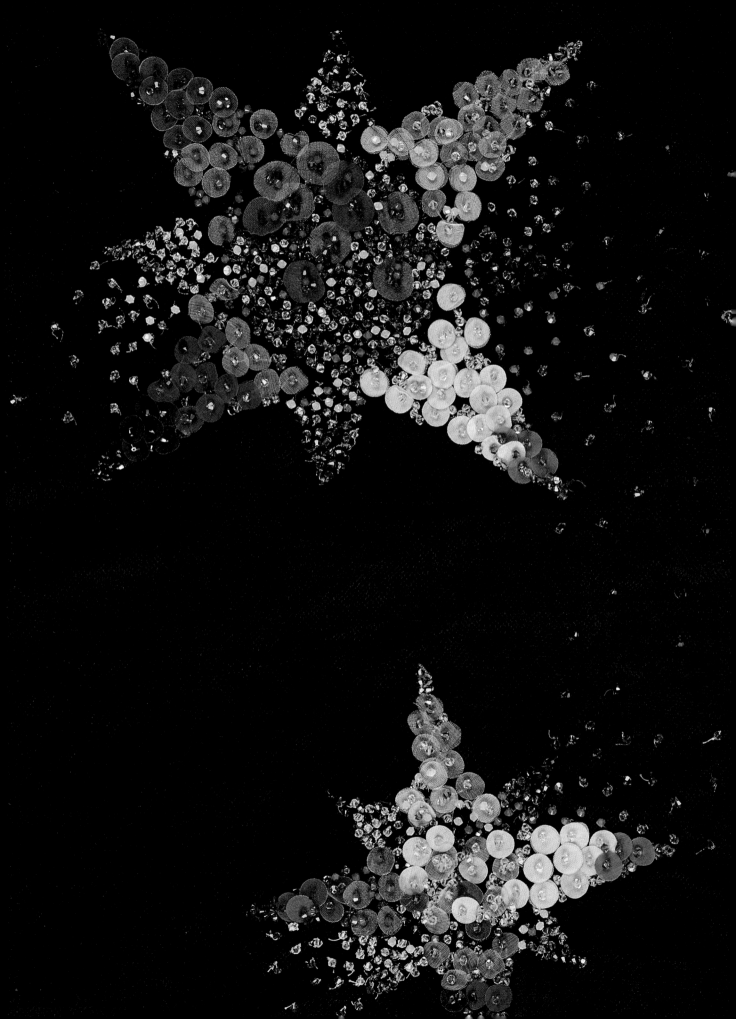

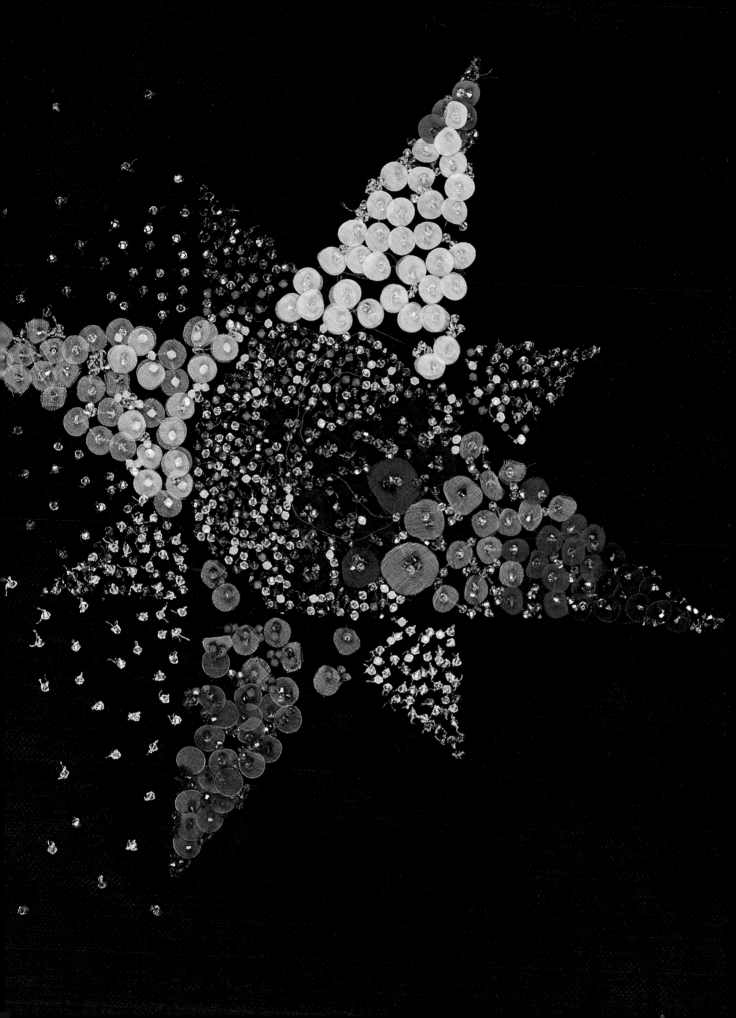

In the early 2000s, Chanel began to hold dedicated runway shows designed to highlight the work of its Métiers d'Art ateliers. Held in a different city every year, these shows call for particular skill and inventiveness. Apart from being a demonstration of skill, embroidery has to be made for accessories – bags, gloves and shoes – designed to coordinate with dresses, suits and coats in what are once again very unexpected materials.

The desire to respect tradition and skills without sticking to a set formula, the talent for innovation that has been the watchword of Lesage since the time of Albert and François, and the advent of new technologies such as laser cutting and 3D printing seem to extend the limits of the possible all the time.

Also with a view to the future, the ateliers are to be moved again in 2020 to a specially designed 'Maison de Mode' at Porte d'Aubervilliers, which Chanel has commissioned from the architect Rudy Ricciotti. This will provide scope for further creativity by the Métiers d'Art embroiderers and ateliers.

But, as in so many other areas where human skills seem to have been overtaken by technological progress, each of the players in Lesage's current story is well aware that the firm's real raison d'être and future originate from a few gestures recorded by Charles-Germain de Saint-Aubin in the late 18th century and the skill of the many invisible hands which, after pricking the sheet of paper, transferring the design in a fine shower of chalk and fixing it on the fabric, began their slow and painstaking work with needle and hook.

opposite   Chanel Fall/Winter 2014–2015 Haute Couture

overleaf, left   Chanel 2013 Cruise 'Versailles'
overleaf, right   Chanel 2014–2015 Cruise 'Dubai'
page 210   Chanel Fall/Winter 2015–2016 Haute Couture
page 211   Chanel Fall/Winter 2017–2018 Ready-to-Wear
page 212   Chanel Spring/Summer 2012 Haute Couture
page 213   Chanel 2015–2016 'Paris in Rome' Métiers d'Art

François Lesage at 13 rue de la Grange-Batelière, Paris, 2001

NOTES

Although Lesage has been the subject of numerous articles over the years, there is one definitive book about the House: Palmer White's *Haute Couture Embroidery: The Art of Lesage* (Simon & Schuster, New York, 1994), translated into French during the same year under the title *Lesage, Maître-Brodeur de la Haute Couture* (Editions du Chêne, Paris). White's book, which was clearly written in collaboration with and under the watchful eye of François Lesage, remains the essential source on all aspects of the history of the House until the end of the 1980s; the present book is hugely indebted to White's work in this respect.

Patrick Mauriès

p. 11 'everything would fall apart': a well-known quote from Madame Necker

p. 16 'that virtually made flamboyance its guiding principle': H. Baudrillart, *Histoire du luxe privé et public*, Paris, 1881, IV, p. 583

p. 19 'but their excess does not help to encourage economy by the poor or virtuous behaviour by the rich': Baudrillart, ibid., p. 655

p. 19 'forty embroidery houses mushroomed almost overnight': Palmer White, *Haute Couture Embroidery: The Art of Lesage*, Simon & Schuster, New York, 1994, p. 25

p. 26 'He felt that life, love and happiness should be pursued elsewhere': White, ibid., p. 33

p. 37 'the eldest of the three sisters, a great perfectionist': White, ibid., p. 47

p. 39 'occasionally fastened by hooks or pop-fasteners, never by a zip': White, ibid., p. 48

p. 51 'to sketch on cotton canvas the place that an embroidery was to occupy': White, ibid., p. 37

p. 57 'to calculate the design of a length of embroidery in relation to the fall of a gown': White, ibid., p. 48

p. 62 'Albert came to fear that soon there would only be nine': White, ibid., p. 58

p. 69 'According to her biographer Meryle Secrest': *Elsa Schiaparelli: A Biography*, London: Fig Tree, 2014

p. 69 'the gulf between the casual and the dressy': Secrest, ibid., p. 77

p. 69 'an artistic masterpiece and a triumph of colour blending': Secrest, ibid., p. 78

p. 80 'plastics, latex, cellophane, rayon crêpe, tulle and knits': White, op. cit., p. 62

p. 80 'and also Albert Lesage's best-ever creations': Palmer White, *Elsa Schiaparelli: Empress of Paris Fashion*, London: Aurum, 1986, pp. 164–170

p. 85 'while ferns adorned their lapels': White, ibid. (*Elsa Schiaparelli*), p. 170

p. 86 'she never repeated herself': an interview with François Lesage in *L'Express*, 8 June 1984, quoted by Secrest, op. cit., p. 198

p. 89 'For 1937, it was 1,551,539 francs': White, *Haute Couture Embroidery*, op. cit., p. 66

p. 97 'he resorted to cord, even string': White, ibid., p. 74

p. 97 'to defy the Nazis in the name of love': White, ibid., p. 67

p. 103 'what could have been a wonderful professional friendship': *La dépêche*, 11 April 2009

p. 107 'on whatever long table happened to be available and sketched': White, *Haute Couture Embroidery*, op. cit., p. 83

p. 111 'François later reported home': White, ibid., p. 86

p. 112 'for whom he designed several ensembles': *L'Officiel de la Mode*, no. 680, 1982, pp. 282–283

p. 112 'where to put the embroidery on Marlene Dietrich, where it was supposed to go': 'François Lesage, artificier de la haute couture', M (*Le Monde*), 27 January 2009

p. 118 'in the search for unusual, unexpected and amusing effects and objects': White, *Haute Couture Embroidery*, op. cit., p. 100

p. 119 'design pieces that resembled Cordoba leather': White, ibid., p. 102

p. 119 'a crinkled nylon gauze which soon became all the rage': White, ibid., p. 102

p. 124 'It had to be sprayed with water every two hours to keep the plants fresh': White, ibid., p. 99

p. 128 'Unlike a machine, the hand knows no limits': White, ibid., p. 108

p. 128 'the mingling of silk thread with straw or cellophane chenille': White, ibid., p. 109

p. 131 'cabochons, Scottish plaids, and plastic feathers': White, ibid., p. 110

p. 136 'turtle shells, crocodiles, tree bark and so on': White, ibid., p. 118

p. 141 'including real gold sheets and velvet on chiffon': White, ibid., p. 124

p. 142 'The collection grew from that': *L'Officiel de la Mode*, no. 680, 1982, pp. 282–283

p. 148 'to pick up the pieces that had been finished in the interval': White, *Haute Couture Embroidery*, op. cit., pp. 32–33

p. 151 'It took 350 hours to embroider each piece': *M* (*Le Monde*), op. cit.

p. 159 'including those from Michonet, piled up at rue de la Grange-Batelière': Veronica Horwell, 'François Lesage', *The Guardian*, 5 December 2011

p. 167 'from then on I never wanted to do anything else': Olivier Michel, 'La broderie française renaît à Madras', *Le Figaro Magazine*, 2 January 2010

p. 170 'a sharing of our strengths and weaknesses': Olivier Michel, ibid.

p. 171 'and the side boxes from an old photo in six weeks': Olivier Michel, ibid.

PICTURE CREDITS

ACKNOWLEDGMENTS

The author and the publisher would like to offer their gratitude and thanks to the following people for their assistance and support in the making of this book:

Lesage   Jean-François Lesage, Caroline Le Borgne, Hubert Barrère, Murielle Lemoine

Chanel   Marie-Louise de Clermont-Tonnerre, Laurence Delamare, Cécile Goddet-Dirles, Nathalie Vibert, Fanny de Kervenoael, Agnès Brisson-Personnaz

Page numbers in *italics* refer
to illustrations.

accessories 62, 79, 156
ACT 3 187, 193
Adrian 112
Alaïa, Azzedine 142
Alix 51 *see also* Grès, Madame
archives 34, 57, 159, 183
Art Deco 57, 80
L'Art du Brodeur
    (Saint-Aubin) *12, 13*

Baccart 16
Balenciaga, Cristóbal
    1950s *108, 114, 116–17*
    1960s *113, 126,* 131, *132–3*
    Lesage relationship 97, 102, 118,
        119, 128
    photographs *130*
    'Théâtre de la Mode'
        exhibition 102
    World War II 98
ballet 33
Balmain, Pierre
    1950s *104, 122–3, 129*
    begins design career 103
    Lesage relationship 103, 118,
        124–5, 128, 141
Barbier, Judith 125
Bardot, Brigitte 124
Barrère, Hubert *192,* 193
Barrioz, Jean 102, 119
Baudrillart, Henri 15–16, 19
beading
    Lunéville *46,* 47, 57
    'soufflé' 57–8
    vermicelli technique 57
Beaton, Cecil *73*
bedroom, Lanvin's *168–9,* 171
Beene, Geoffrey 148
Bégué, René 103, 118
Benjamin, Walter 19
Bérard, Christian *68,* 70, *83, 85,* 102
Berthault, Jean Louis 111–12
Bettina (model) 124
Blass, Bill 148
Bohan, Marc 131
Bouvet de Lozier, Simone 25, 51,
    111, 115
Boyer, Charles 111

Breton, André 33
Buffet-Picabia, Gabrielle 69
bullion 80

Callot Soeurs 19, 37, 118
Cardin, Pierre 128
Carven, Marie-Louise 118
cellulose acetate 102, 119
Ceretti, Vittoria *188*
Chambre Syndicale de la Haute
    Couture 79, 98, 102
Chanel
    1920s 34
    1980s *154, 156–7, 161, 172, 174,* 177
    1990s 174, *175–6,* 177, *179*
    2000s 207
    2010s *162–3,* 177, *180–2, 184–6,*
        188–91, 194–7, 200–3, 206,
        208–13
    atelier purchases 173–4, 177–8
    Lagerfeld 148, 174, 193
    Lesage relationship 160, 174–8,
        183, 193, 207
    Métiers d'Art 187, 193, 207
    motifs & styles 174
    Paraffection 174, 177–8, 183, 193
    Spring/Summer 2017 *2*
Chanel, Gabrielle 174
Chareau, Pierre 45
Christofle 16–19
Cocteau, Jean 70, *72–3,* 102
Colbert, Claudette 112
Comité Colbert 13, 156
Coromandel designs 174, *179*
Courrèges 128
craft guilds 15
Crahay, Jules-François 131

Dadaism 33
Dali, Salvador 70
De Havilland, Olivia 112
de La Fressange, Inès *161*
De la Renta, Oscar 148
Deharme, Lise 85
Deniot, Jean-Louis 170
Despense-Railly, Berthe de 49, 105
Despense-Railly, Marie-Louise
    family 90, 98, 105–7
    Maison Lesage work 62, 118
    marriage to Albert 51, 55–7
    photographs *50*

Desrues 173
Dessès, Jean 118, 125
Diaz, Elsa 112, 115
Dietrich, Marlene *110,* 112
Dior 131, 178, *204*
Dior, Christian 97, 101, 103, 121–4
Doucet, Jacques 19, 34, 39
Dunand, Jean 45

economic crises 61, 159–60, 187
Exhibition of Decorative Arts
    33, 57
exhibitions, Lesage 156

Fath, Jacques 97, 98, 118, 124
Favot, Louis 115
Favot, Paul 49
Fini, Léonor 70
flapper dresses 47
Fortuny, Mariano 141
Frank, Jean-Michel 45
furnishing 159, 170–1, 187

Galeries Lafayette 69
Galliano, John 178
Garcia, Jacques 170
Gardner, Ava 112
Givenchy, Hubert de 125, 141
Goma, Michel 131
Goossens 174, 183
Graf, François-Joseph 170
Grange, Jacques 170
Greffulhe, Élisabeth, Countess *56*
Grès, Madame 51, 98, 102
Griffe, Jacques 125
Grube von Klewitz, Gisela 165
guilds 15

Hachette 23, 167
Hadid, Gigi *184–5*
Hamelin 159, 170
Hardin, Ondria *197*
Harlow, Shalom *175*
Haute Couture, beginnings of 19
Hayworth, Rita 111–12
Head, Edith 112
Heim, Jacques 118
Hermès 19
Herrera, Carolina 148
Hillingso, Lars 159
Hollywood 111–12

India *164*, 167–71
Irene 112

Jacobs, Marc 178
Jean-Louis 111–12

Kahn, Charles 69
Kelly, Grace *117*
Klein, Calvin 148

Lacroix, Christian
  1980s *150*, 151, *152–3*
  closure 160
  Lesage relationship 119, 151, 155
  Schiaparelli collection 178
Lagerfeld, Karl *see also* Chanel
  1990s *175*
  2010s *149*
  begins at Chanel 148, 174
  Lesage relationship 174, 177–8,
    187, 193
  photographs *184–5*
Lanvin 131
Lanvin, Jeanne *168–9*, 171
Lars Paris 159
Lelong, Lucien 95, 98, 102, 103, 118
Lemarié 174, 183
Lemoine, Murielle 187
Lesage, Adèle 23, 107
Lesage, Albert
  business after Wall Street
    Crash 62
  business after WWII 102
  childhood 23, 25
  death 115
  early career 25, 33
  marriage to Marie-Louise 51, 55
  Michonet relationship 34, 61
  photographs *24, 96*
  USA 25–6, 89–90
  work for Schiaparelli 79–80, 86
  work for Vionnet 47, 57
  World War II 90, 95, 97–8
Lesage, Christiane *56, 61, 96, 107*
Lesage creation *120, 146*
Lesage, François
  on the art of embroidery 128
  awards 156
  begins leadership of
    Maison 118
  birth & childhood *56, 61, 105–7*

Comité Colbert 13, 156
  death 178
  as designer 156
  early work 107
  family 167
  innovations 128–31, 174–7,
    187
  on inspiration 142
  meets Barrère 193
  photographs *6–7, 96, 106, 214*
  return to France 115
  on Schiaparelli 86
  USA 109, 111–12, 115, 148
Lesage, Gustave 23
Lesage Intérieurs 187
Lesage, Jean-François
  birth & childhood 165–7
  on his father 107, 167
  India 167, 170–1
  Lesage Intérieurs 187
  photographs *166*
Lesage, Jean-Louis *56, 61, 90, 95,*
  98, 105
Lesage, Marie-Louise *see*
  Despense-Railly, Marie-Louise
Lesage school *146, 159*, 187
Los Angeles 111
Lucky (model) 124
Lunéville beading *46, 47*, 57

mainteuses 47
Maison Lesage *see also*
  archives; techniques
  accessories 62, 79, 156
  after Albert's death 118
  Balenciaga relationship 97,
    102, 118, 119, 128
  Balmain relationship 103, 118,
    124–5, 128, 141
  Chanel relationship 160, 174–8,
    183, 193, 207
  Dior relationship 121–4
  economic crises 62, 159–60
  exhibitions 156
  Fath relationship 124
  furnishing 159, 170–1, 187
  Givenchy relationship 125, 141
  India 170–1
  Klein relationship 148
  Lacroix relationship 151
  Prêt-à-Porter growth 155–6

Saint Laurent relationship
  135–6, 141, 151
Scherrer relationship 141
Schiaparelli relationship
  79–80, 85, 89, 118–19
textiles business 102, 118, 187
'Théâtre de la Mode'
  exhibition 102
USA 89–90, 109, 111–12, 115,
  147–8
working methods 142, 151,
  198–9
World War II 90, 95, 97
Maison Michel 174, 183
Marino, Peter 170
Marshall Field and Company 25
Massaro 174, 183
material shortages due to war 97,
  98, 101, 109
McCardell, Claire 147
McFadden, Mary 148
Mendl, Lady (Elsie de Wolfe) *66*
Messner, Maria 187, 193
Métiers d'Art 187, 193, 207
Michonet
  19th century *10, 17, 18, 27–32*
  20th century *14, 20–1, 22, 35, 48*
  Lesage relationship 34, 55–7, 61
  Vionnet relationship 45
Michonet, Albert 19, 34, 51, 57
Molyneux, Edward 103
Molyneux, Juan-Pablo 170
Monroe, Marilyn 112
Mont-Dore 90, 95, 107
Montenay, Françoise 173
Mori, Hanae 141
Mugler, Thierry 148
Musée des Arts Décoratifs 58,
  101–2, *168–9*, 171

Napoleon 16
Necker, Madame (Suzanne
  Curchod) 11
New Look 101, 118, 121
Niane, Katoucha *138*

Orry-Kelly 112
Oudenot, Colette 165

Pantin 183–7
Paquin 19

Paraffection 174, 177–8, 183, 193
passementerie 19, 62
Patou 34, 131, 151
Pavlovsky, Bruno 174
Peregalli, Roberto 170
petites mains 13
Picabia, Francis 70
Piguet, Robert 97, 118
Pillement, Jean 124–5
Pinto, Alberto 170
Poiret, Paul 34, 39, 51, 69
pouncing 46, 170
Powel, Christian 90
Prêt-à-Porter 135, 147, 148, 155,
    174, 187

Rabanne, Paco 128
Rao, Sandeep 170
Ready-to-Wear *see* Prêt-à-Porter
Rébé 103, 118
Redfern 19, 34
Reily, Kate 37
rhodoid 119
Rochas, Marcel 98, 118
Roehm, Carolyne 148
Rogers, Millicent *87*
Rouff, Maggy 98

Saint-Aubin, Charles-Germain de
    12, 13, 207
Saint Laurent, Yves
    1970s 136, *137*
    1980s 136, *137–40,* 141, *143–5*
    1990s *134*
    Lesage relationship 124, 131,
        135–6, 141, 151
    retirement 160
    Rive Gauche 135
    Schiaparelli homage 136
Savouret, Patrick 170
Scherrer, Jean-Louis 131, 141, 156
Schiaparelli, Elsa
    1930s *78, 87, 92, 93*
    Astrology collection 66–7, *71,*
        76, 85–6
    begins design career 69
    Circus collection *64, 84,* 85
    'Cocteau' coat *72–3, 74–5*
    Commedia dell'Arte
        collection 86
    return to Europe 65–9

first meeting with
    Albert Lesage 26
Lacroix collection 178
Lesage relationship 79–80, 85,
    89, 118–19
Music collection 80, *88*
Pagan collection *77, 81,* 85
perfumes 85, 89
Phoebus cape *82–3*
portrait *68*
post-World War II *100,* 118–19
'soufflé' beads 58
style 69–70
'Théâtre de la Mode' exhibition
    102
World War II *91,* 95–7
Schlumberger, Jean 85
Scott, L'Wren 178
Secrest, Meryle 69
Shivakumar, Malavika 170
Sirakian, Edouard 109
Sun, Fei Fei *157*
surrealism 33

Talosel 102
tambour beading *see* Lunéville
    beading techniques
    Albert Lesage 80
    François Lesage on 128
    Lunéville beading *46, 47,* 57
    new technology 207
    'soufflé' beads 57–8
    thermopasted film 141
    vermicelli 57
    war shortages 97
    work for Balenciaga 119
    work for Balmain 124
    work for Dessès 125
    work for Fath 124
    work for Saint Laurent
        136, 141
    work for Schiaparelli
        80, 85–6
Terry, Emilio 102
textiles 102, 118, 187, 193
'Théâtre de la Mode'
    exhibition 101–2
thermopasted film 141
Thiers, Adolphe 15
Tierney, Gene 112
Touchagues, Louis 102

Toussaint, Mr 90
Trémolet, Gérard 156
Triolet, Elsa 136
Turner, Lana 112
tweed 187, *188–91,* 193

Ungaro, Emanuel 131
USA 25–6, 89–90, 109, 111–12, 115,
    147–8

Valentino 178, *205*
Vastrakala *164,* 170
Vauthier, Alexandre 178
Vautrin, Line 102
Veil, Simone *149*
vermicelli technique 57
Versailles 1973 show 148
Vertès, Marcel 70, 85
Viard, Virginie 177, 193
Vincent 37
Vionnet
    1920s *40*
    1930s *36, 41–3, 52–3, 59–60, 63*
    motifs & styles 45, 47, 57, 58
Vionnet, Madeleine 37, *38,* 39, 47,
    51, 55, 58
Vogue 69, *73, 83, 85, 87, 156*
Vuitton 19, 178

Wall Street Crash 61
Wendt de Kerlor, William 25, 65
White, Palmer
    on Albert Lesage 25, 26
    on Balenciaga 119
    on François Lesage 107, 119, 128
    on Klein 148
    on Lesage business 62, 80, 89,
        97, 151
    on Marie-Louise
        Despense-Railly 51
    on Michonet 34
    on Rébé 103
    on Schiaparelli 118
    on Vionnet 37, 39
    on Worth 19
Wolfe, Elsie de *66*
World War I 25, 51
World War II 90, 95, 97–8
Worth, Charles Frederick 19, 34,
    54, 56, 99
Wu, Jason 178

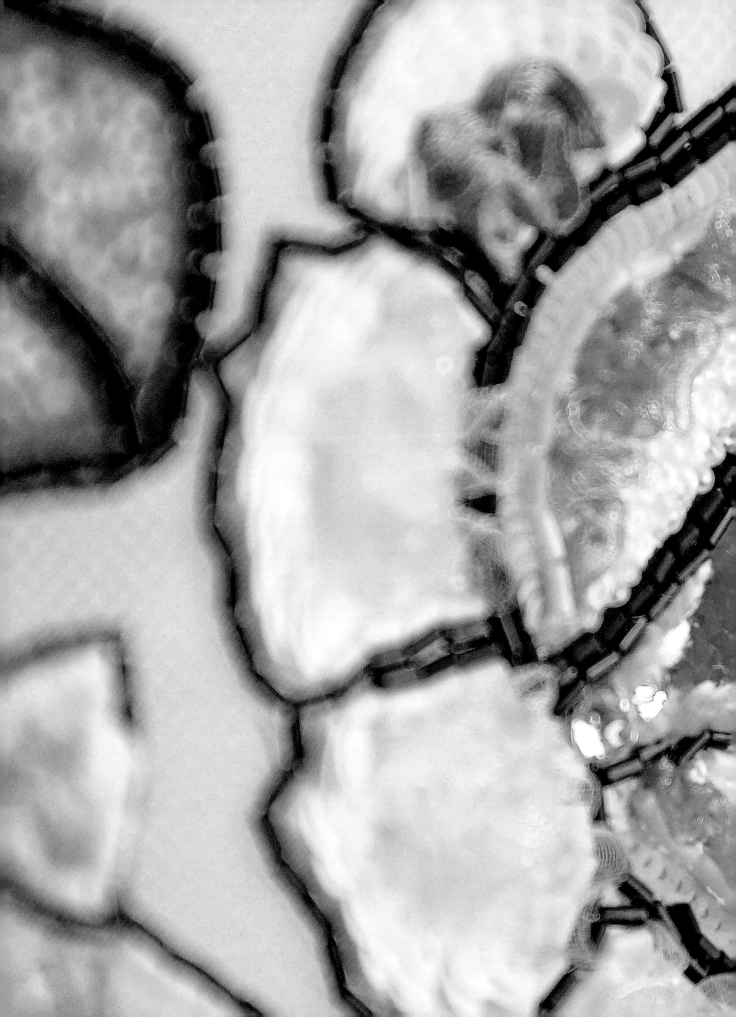

On the cover Chanel Fall/Winter 1983 Haute Couture © Olivier Saillant
p. 2 Chanel Spring/Summer 2017 Haute Couture
pp. 4–5 Lesage's atelier in Pantin, Paris
pp. 6–7 François Lesage in the former atelier at 13 rue de la Grange-Batelière, Paris
pp. 222–223 Study piece from the Lesage school of Haute Couture embroidery

Main text translated from the French by Lorna Dale

First published in the United Kingdom in 2020 by
Thames & Hudson Ltd, 181A High Holborn, London WC1V 7QX

First published in the United States of America in 2020 by
Thames & Hudson Inc., 500 Fifth Avenue, New York, New York 10110

Reprinted 2022

Interior book layout and typography by Studio Mathias Clottu
Initial letters designed by Adrien Vasquez

British Library Cataloguing-in-Publication Data
A catalogue record for this book is available from the British Library

Library of Congress Control Number 2018932304

ISBN 978-0-500-02153-8

Printed and bound in China by Artron

Be the first to know about our new releases,
exclusive content and author events by visiting
thamesandhudson.com
thamesandhudsonusa.com
thamesandhudson.com.au